The Invisible Conversations™
with
Your Aging Parents

Shannon A. White

ISBN: 978-1-937829-17-9

*Dedicated to families who yearn for deeper
connection during all stages of life.*

The Invisible Conversations ™ with Your Aging Parents

Table of Contents

Part 1 - Getting Started 1

- Introduction 3

- What's on the Minds of Older Adults? 3

- The Visible and the Invisible: Possibilities and Challenges 5

- Where Are Things Right Now? Taking an Initial Inventory 9

- Documents 9

Part 2 - Preparing for What is to Come 11

- Documents 13

  Living Wills, Medical Power of Attorneys, DNR, Last Will and Testament,
  Medical and Drug Information Sheet

- Healthcare Concerns…Being Your Parent's Patient Advocate 20

- Where to Live? 26

- Money 30

- When Driving is No Longer Safe 35

- Aging and Alcoholism 37

- When Mom or Dad is Dating 40

Part 3 - Caregiving 43

- Who is the Caregiver? 45

- Adult Children as Caregivers 47

- Invisible Conversations with Outside Caregivers 51

- Communicating with Siblings 54

- Loss and Grief 56

● Remembering, Before it's Too Late 60

● Completing the Relationship…Unfinished Business.. 63

● Preparation for Death... 67

● Caring for the Caregiver 71

● Protecting Your Loved One... 74

Part 4 - Practical Considerations.. 77

● How and When to Begin These Conversations 79

● Why Some Conversations Are Invisible... 81

● Next Steps 87

● Resources 88

● Acknowledgements... 90

● About the Author 91

Part 1

Getting Started

Introduction

What's on the Minds of Older Adults?

A dult children want to make sure their parents are happy, healthy, and peaceful as they age. They want their parents to be able to live out the rest of their lives with dignity and in accordance with their wishes. And adult children want to ensure their parents have as many choices as possible regarding their care when looking into the future.

The leading edge of the Baby Boom generation is becoming a very different generation of older adults. Their needs and concerns are making an impact on current legislation and shaping future trends in healthcare choices.

What's on the minds of seniors? According to research done by AARP in 2011 with adults over age 50:

- Four in ten adults 50+ say that health care issues are the top problems or challenges facing mid-life and older adults in their state.
- Over one-third cites economic issues as the largest challenge.
- About 80% of adults 50+ worry about one or more financial issues.
- Public assistance benefits, maintaining finances, and lifestyle in retirement are worries for two-thirds.
- Over 80% of adults 50+ worry about one or more consumer protection issues.
- At least two-thirds express concern about protecting themselves against consumer fraud and unfair and deceptive business practices.
- Staying in their own homes as they age is important to adults 50+. Nearly all say it is important to have long-term care services that allow people to remain in their own homes.
- Four in five support shifting funds used for nursing home care to community-based care.
  (http://assets.aarp.org/rgcenter/general/voices-america-dreams-challenges-national.pdf based on 29,000 adults)

Studies also show:

- Most people expect their families to carry out their wishes about end-of-life care — yet 75 percent admit they have never clearly articulated what those wishes are. And our families are afraid to ask them.

While older adults may be clear about their needs, the conversations with their adult children about those needs may not be occurring. Research conducted by caregiverstress.com shows "nearly one-third of adults in the U.S. have a major communication obstacle with their parents that stems from continuation of the parent-child role. That same dynamic—and others—can come into play as well for older adults dealing with their adult children." This book helps bring those conversations out into the open so that you can ensure your parents' needs are met with compassion and dignity in their final years.

The Visible and the Invisible: Possibilities and Challenges

We communicate with others through conversations. They are spoken and they are unspoken. They are verbal and they are nonverbal. They are visible and they are invisible. I use the term, "Invisible Conversations" ™ to describe all of those conversations which are not communicated with the intended person or people. Oftentimes these conversations stay up in your head and don't come out of your mouth.

The motivations for NOT having these conversations may be conscious or unconscious. For the most part, they are purposely NOT spoken to the intended recipient. Sometimes they are spoken indirectly to others who are not involved. Invisible conversations leave you with many emotions including: anger, fear, worry, sadness, and grief. These conversations and their accompanying feelings take up a lot of space in your brain creating distracting chatter and leave you with a lack of autonomy both internally and externally.

These invisible conversations cover most sensitive topics with which we are uncomfortable due to their nature. They deal with emotionally charged issues which surround sex, finances, religion, values, culture, and end of life decisions. Invisible conversations may deal with the past, present, or future. They can last for a few minutes or for a lifetime. Invisible conversations happen between those closest to us and those whom we barely know. But they affect everyone involved.

Some examples of when these invisible conversations may come to the surface between adult children and their aging parents include: when you see your parents begin to decline and become frail; when Mom gets a life-altering diagnosis; when there are questions about how Dad's care will be handled and by whom; when the question is raised over where Mom will live; when there is struggle over providing care and estate planning between siblings, step-families, and unmarried partnerships in the older and younger generation; when an adult son moves in to care for Mom and other siblings think he may be taking financial advantage of her; when Dad wants to date again after Mom's death; when death is nearing and there are unresolved issues from long ago.

Here's my story…

I lived in invisible conversations with my father for over 30 years. They wreaked havoc in my life. They kept me living in a script which prevented me from authentically connecting with him and affected my overall personal growth and self-esteem. They also kept me from succeeding in romantic relationships with men and from facing authority figures as an adult at work.

Back when I was in my early 30's my father was dying of cancer. He was 57 years old and his cancer was back, for the second time. The horrific end reality of the disease was plain enough to understand that my therapist encouraged me to go and complete my "unfinished business" with him before he died. She told me, "You can do it at the grave, but it's much better to do it while he's still living."

I was terrified. From the time I was very little, I had always been afraid of my father. He always seemed larger than life, and he had a temper which I experienced regularly. One specific physical incident with him when I was 13 years old had left its mark on me so deeply that I had been stuck in that moment ever since then, and didn't even realize it.

Our relationship had been full of invisible conversations which kept us from ever being real with one another. The thought of going to say my "good-byes" was beyond what I thought I could do. I was stuck in the emotional life of that 13-year-old, but in a 30-year-old body. In addition, I had to wade through my perceptions of an unspoken, long-standing family rule that you "don't do anything to upset Dad." My reality was you never knew exactly what would upset him, so that meant doing nothing or there could be physical or emotional consequences.

I knew my therapist was right, however, and I traveled a distance to the state where he lived. When I walked into his living room, he was sitting quietly on the couch. He wasn't able to speak at that point because he had a laryngectomy. I sat down next to him, looked him in the eye, and quietly but confidently said, "Dad, I have always been afraid of you. But I'm here to tell you that I'm OK. I'm fine. The things which happened between us have not held me back. What's important now is that there is love, and peace, and forgiveness." I had never spoken to him with such truth before that moment. He looked deep into my eyes for a brief moment, blew me a kiss, and closed his eyes.

Moments later, I walked onto his front porch. In that moment, I felt myself mature from the day of that painful event back at age 13 to my present age. I got into my car and as I drove through the four states back to my home, I dry heaved most of the way. I felt like slabs of concrete were breaking up inside of me and all of the fear and anger of those early years were erupting forth like a volcano. With each gag reflex I felt freer and freer. Finally, there was nothing left and I was at peace.

Bringing that conversation from invisible to visible was one of the most spiritual experiences I have ever had. My dad died two weeks later, but I was able to attend and even speak at his funeral with gratitude for his life. No longer was I the fearful girl who was afraid to stand up to authority figures. I had grown up to be a woman who could speak her truth with love.

Thank you, Dad.

As I started writing this book, and conducting interviews with people in the field of eldercare and those many brave people who love day in and day out, caring for their aging loved ones, I knew I needed to have more conversations with my OWN mother. You might call it a kind of a "practice what you preach" scenario. At age 75, she had just undergone major surgery. I knew at one point (10 years before then) she had asked me to be her Health Care Power of Attorney and had sent me her forms to keep on file. Since all of this information about having conversations with your parents was fresh in my head, I asked her about it. "Am I still your health care agent?" She quickly responded, "Well, I didn't want to tell you, but I changed it (my Health Care Power of Attorney) this time around." "OK," I said quickly. Then I asked, "How come you didn't tell me?" She said, "I didn't want to hurt your feelings."

Uh oh...an invisible conversation.

Evidently I had not created a situation where my mother felt she could tell me she had changed her mind. This was a great opportunity to help ease her mind, to encourage her to be able to tell me what she wanted and needed to, and to let her know that whatever she decides about her life and her care in the future is OK with me. It's even better than OK. It's the right thing to do.

Parent-child dynamics and sibling dynamics are based on patterns of behavior and experiences which often fail to acknowledge the changes which occur over time in the individuals involved. Everything and everyone may be different, yet many often stick to the operation manual of an earlier time and place.

By the time aging parents are transitioning into the later stages of their lives, some of the invisible conversations with their adult children may have been in operation for decades. Those who have the tools to express their feelings, needs, and desires are better able to deal with the aging and dying process in the short and long term. This is true for the person facing end of life as well as family members, caregivers, or friends.

For some, the days of being able to have meaningful conversations have passed. Being present with compassion and care is the task at hand.

❀ ❀ ❀ ❀ ❀

Betsy was talking about her difficult and sometimes very frustrating journey with her mother who has dementia. She said one of the things which gives her great strength and keeps her sane when everything seems to be impossible is a saying from a book called "Simple Truths: Clear and Gentle Guidance on the Big Issues of Life," by Kent Nerburn:

"Your heart is revealed by the way you treat your elders." *Reprinted with permission of New World Library, Novato, CA. www.newworldlibrary.com.*

Betsy says, "This is not about my mother. It's about doing the right thing for another human being...We're all capable of finding that place of compassion and we have to find it."

❀ ❀ ❀ ❀ ❀

She's right. This journey is as much about your own development as it is about those for whom you love and care. This experience may require you to muster a whole new set of skills you never knew you had. It may call on you to draw from a deep well of courage that has been untapped before now or to develop the practice of patience. You may have to develop new strengths on the spot. You will be called upon to be the best you can be.

I am writing this book not only because of my own experiences with my parents but also because, as an ordained minister for over 20 years, I have been witness to countless families going through the aging and dying processes with a loved one. I have served in three congregations, in a nursing home, and several hospitals as chaplain. I have walked through this journey with extraordinary individuals who are aging and facing the end of their lives. Some have done it with joy and peace and others with some reluctance and struggle. I have also stood by spouses, adult children, and caregivers as their aging loved ones have received diagnoses and courageously fought long or short-term illnesses. I have been privileged to be present around bedsides as last words have been spoken with loved ones. I have also had the sad task of telling families their loved one has died.

I have been present with families who have been able to say everything they needed to say and with others who have multiple "invisible conversations" which have been in operation for decades. My experience tells me those who have the tools to express their feelings, needs, and desires are better able to deal with the aging and dying process. This is true for the person facing end of life as well as family members, caregivers, or friends.

Some have asked me and others in my field how we are able to be around death, dying, and grief on such a regular basis. I have considered it a privilege to have been invited into the lives of so many families both at times of both celebration as well as pain. The dying process is very human. When a person or family is dealing with the prelude to death and they have dropped the masks they have hidden behind in their everyday lives, it is truly "holy ground." May you have many of those moments as well.

A final note on how to use this book. This material is meant for you to reference as needed. You may not need to read straight through, from beginning to end. Use it as you need it. Refer to it before the conversations you need to have, or bring it along and read it together with your parent. Sometimes, having something else to focus on, or reading someone else's story and asking them if they relate is a good way to get important information. However you use it, may you and your parents forge a deeper connection as you journey together.

Where Are Things Right Now? Taking an Initial Inventory

Wherever you are in this journey is exactly the right place. You may be well on your way, equipped with knowledge of and agreement on plans, preparations, and expectations. Your parent may have some of the necessary documents on file from a long time ago, but has taken a turn for the worse and it's time to review them and make some additional decisions. Your parent may be at a crisis point in care and you may have no knowledge of what his wishes are.

This book will help you address the issues and to ask the questions which are needed at this stage of life. To begin, it's important to take an inventory of where you are right now. The following inventory is meant to be a map for your own purposes to help you know where you might need to focus some additional attention in planning and conversation. Certainly every situation is different and has special nuances. So, as the saying goes, "take what you want and leave the rest."

(Note: For these purposes, I am going to use the singular form of parent, even though you may be dealing with the needs of both of your parents. Use this as a worksheet and change it as needed.)

Documents

Does your parent have or have they designated:

      Power of Attorney (financial)   yes, no, I don't know
      Medical Power of Attorney (Health Care Agent)   yes, no, I don't know
      Living Will or Quality of Life Drafting   yes, no, I don't know
      DNR Orders (Do Not Resuscitate), if desired   yes, no, I don't know
      Last Will and Testament   yes, no, I don't know

Decisions:

- Is your parent cognitively able to have conversations about his present circumstances and his future?

- Have you decided which family member will be the first point of contact for decisions both now and in the future?

- Are you dealing with a recent diagnosis? If yes, what do you know about the particular ailment?

- Do you know how she is feeling about what is happening to her?

- Have you settled living arrangements both now and in the future? Is she aware of the decisions? How does she feel about the decisions being made?

Support:

- Does your parent have a support system in place? (Some examples are: house of worship, friends, neighbors, caregivers.) If yes, do you have contact information for each individual/group?

- Do you have a support system in place for yourself? Who are they?

- Are your siblings up to date and in agreement with the current situation and decisions which have been made?

- Do you need additional help right now?

If in reviewing any of these questions you find yourself getting overwhelmed, that's OK. This book will take you step by step through the process and some of the decisions you will need to make. If you were able to give answers to most or all of the questions above, keep reading…there is much more information in the coming chapters.

Part 2

Preparing for What is to Come

Documents

What does life look like today for you and your aging parent? What is life going to look like in the next month? Year? Five years? Decade? Are you prepared? What information do you need to get today so that you have as much support and help as possible? These are the documents your aging parent needs to have on hand right now:

Advanced Directives for Medical Care

Thinking and talking with loved ones about how you want to be cared for at the end of life is important. The best way to ensure your healthcare wishes, beliefs, and values are honored is through the use of what are called Advanced Directives for Medical Care. These documents may be state-specific, but usually include: a living will and a medical proxy/health care power of attorney.

A. Living Wills

A living will is a legal document which outlines your decisions regarding your medical treatment if you are no longer able to make decisions due to catastrophic injury or illness. It is enacted by medical triggers. You are asked if you wish to receive life support in the form of: CPR (with electric shock), artificial ventilation, and artificial nutrition. You can also designate whether you wish to be an organ donor.

Each State Department of Health website provides documents which you can download and complete without the assistance of an attorney (for more, see Resources section). Your state may have specific requirements including signatures of several witnesses and/or notarization of your signature on the documents. If you are scheduled to have surgery or a major procedure, many hospitals will also make sure you have a living will to be in effect for that procedure. If you do not already have a living will, they will ask you questions before your operation/procedure.

Some attorneys encourage obtaining a "Quality of Life Drafting" rather than a living will. This is because living wills are enacted by medical triggers and don't always take into consideration other issues which may come into play before a catastrophic incident. For example, some people might not want to receive CPR if they have dementia and suffer a severe stroke, leaving them paralyzed. Others would want CPR in that case. A quality of life drafting can offer more nuance to complex situations.

The questions come down to: What kind of quality of life do you want at the end of your life? Have you discussed your thoughts and decisions with your family? How do they feel about your decisions? I have stood around many hospital beds with families of both young and old patients who are agonizing over whether or not to "pull the plug" and end the life of their loved one. Many times there have been differing opinions among family members over what should be done, especially due to differing religious beliefs. By completing these documents, you help relieve your family from having to make additional traumatic decisions in the face of the tremendous pain they are already experiencing. You also help eliminate possible conflicts among family members, because you have been clear about your wishes.

❀　❀　❀　❀　❀

Regina says she's on a bit of an educational crusade for other people to try and find a comfort level with living wills. "There are a few people that think living wills are like wills and you keep them at the bank. You don't." Regina keeps a copy of her living will in her kitchen posted on her wall along with her other paperwork. She also gives copies to everyone who is important in her life. "If you talk to the people who are around me they'll be able to tell you exactly how I feel."

It's important to note that you can change your living will anytime while you are still competent. Keep these documents on file at your home (in an easy to find place), house of worship, your doctor's office, and with friends.

Questions to ask your parent (in addition to those found in a living will document).

- Do you have a living will or a quality of life drafting?
- What are your feelings about being on life support?
- Do your religious beliefs influence your thoughts about it?
- What would be your greatest concern if you were to experience a catastrophic accident or event?
- How would you want us as your family to respond?
- Is there anyone you know who had treatment at the end of life that you would or would not like for yourself?
- Do all of my siblings know your wishes? Why or why not?

B. Health Care Proxy/Health Care Agent/Medical Power of Attorney Designation

A medical power of attorney/health care proxy/surrogate is the person whom you designate to make medical decisions on your behalf if you are no longer able to do so. The determination of incapacitation is made by a medical professional. A medical power of attorney should be a person you trust and who knows your healthcare wishes. The person may not agree with your wishes, but he must be willing to carry them out. This person should also live near you. At some point he may need to act on your behalf in an emergency and then in an on-going basis. You should also appoint an alternate as a back-up in case of emergencies.

Many people who have been through family situations requiring the use of a medical power of attorney say it's much easier to designate one person than to have a team or even two people together. If you choose one of your adult children as your medical power of attorney, it's best to tell your other children why you've made that choice so that there is no confusion. At the point when decisions need to be made on your behalf, you can encourage family discussion, but the final medical decisions will be that of the designee based on your wishes as stated in your documents. However, even if you've made your decisions clear, it doesn't mean there won't be differing opinions. One caregiver who has been through this situation with many families says, "You may still get tough situations where there will be one adult child who may be in disagreement and will hold out from removing life support." If you have made your desires known in this legal document, however, you lessen the chances of serious conflict among your loved ones.

Questions to consider with your parent:

- With whom do you feel most comfortable handling your medical decisions if something happens to you?
- Does that person know you're chosen him?
- Have you made this designation on any signed document?
- Do all of my siblings know your wishes? Why or Why not?

C. DNR or Do Not Resuscitate Order, (if desired)

A DNR order instructs medical professionals not to perform CPR or emergency treatment to restart your heart or lungs when your heartbeat or breathing stops. This is a separate document in your medical file and may be signed by you, your Health Care Proxy or physician. In hospitals, DNR's are listed on the medical chart. In some states these orders need to be made for both hospital and non-hospital situations. Otherwise, emergency personnel are required by law to provide CPR if your heart stops when you outside a medical facility. Upon entering your home, an EMT will look first for a pink sheet called "Patient Orders for Life Sustaining Treatment" or POLST before beginning life-saving treatment. (In some states these documents are called Medical Orders for Life Sustaining Treatment or MOLST). Special bracelets are also used as a signal to let emergency care providers know you have this type of DNR in place. You can also cancel a DNR order, if you choose at any point while you are able.

Many people who have lived with terminal illnesses choose to have a DNR. If they have made peace with the fact that they are dying, many don't want to have their lives prolonged further.

✿ ✿ ✿ ✿ ✿

Regina's husband, Ron, had Parkinson's disease. He was very clear that when the end of his life came, he did not want to be taken to the emergency room and given life support. Regina says living will information needs to be communicated to everyone who has caregiving responsibilities for your loved one as well. "If you're at home and if you have a caregiver with that person, they need to know that's (living will) there.

✿ ✿ ✿ ✿ ✿

Questions to consider with your parent:

- What do you want to have happen if your heart stops?

- Is there any occasion where you would or would not want CPR to be given?
- Have you had detailed conversations with your health care proxy/medical power of attorney regarding your wishes?

D. Last Will and Testament/Living Trusts

People who have assets they want to pass on to survivors need to have a last will and testament. This document names a person, known as an executor (also known as a personal representative, in some states), who will be responsible for distributing any assets, and real, and personal property after the person dies. An executor can be a family member, bank trustee, attorney, or friend…whomever the person chooses and trusts. Having an attorney draw up your will is not mandatory, but it is strongly recommended so you can ensure the requirements of your state are met. Without a will, your remaining property, after debts and funeral expenses are paid, is considered "intestate." In most jurisdictions, the state will take charge and direct any remaining assets to the surviving spouse (majority), to the children, and to their heirs as they determine.

❈ ❈ ❈ ❈ ❈

As an Estates and Trusts attorney, Jacqueline deals with clients who have substantial assets. "As clients age, the conversation changes if they develop a serious illness." Jacqueline works with clients to fund what are called revocable trusts to make sure that the spouse's assets are taken care of and that their health care instructions are in place. "We would ask how immediate or how serious the condition is and how quickly things need to be done. So if it's an early diagnosis of Alzheimer's, how quickly they are expected to get worse? If it's Parkinson's or a serious cancer diagnosis, what's the prognosis? How much time do we have to make changes and what do they want to do?"

One of Jacqueline's clients is in his 70's and has terminal cancer. "We sat at his bedside. He knew he was dying soon and yet his mind was good. He wanted to make a total revamp of his estate planning documents to make sure that his wife was taken care of, and to provide cash bequests to a number of friends who have been particularly kind to him especially since his diagnosis."

❈ ❈ ❈ ❈ ❈

In the event that any of your heirs are currently disabled or may become disabled, you may consider a "Contingent Supplemental Needs Trust." This kind of trust allows for funds to be provided if publicly funded benefits are not sufficient for their care.

Elder Law attorneys can also help interpret state specific laws impacting older adults. They help with advanced care directives and other legal documents as well.

Try This:

Encourage your parents to gather all their important documents in one safe place and create a sheet with all of their account numbers and passwords. These simple actions alleviate scrambling to find them after a loved one's death. Documents to consider including are: Insurance policies, credit card statements, banking records, retirement/pension statements with beneficiary information, tax records, and deeds to property, stock certificates, marriage and divorce papers, titles to vehicles. Then, make sure someone knows where is stored!

Questions to consider with your parent:

- Do you feel confident in your current doctors, attorney, and financial advisor?
- Who has access/how does one get access to your documents at the appropriate time?
- Who has a copy of your Last Will and Testament?
- Who is your executor?
- Are you comfortable talking to us about what is in your will so that we all understand, plan for, and support your decisions both now and after you've gone?
- Do you have any other financial concerns that you want to express?
- What kind of legacy do you want to leave? How can we help support that vision?
- Do you have any current financial concerns about any of your children?
- Do you have any financial concerns about any of us upon your death?
- What would you hope would happen for us as a family after your death?

E. Power of Attorney

This is the person you designate to take over all of your legal and financial matters when you are no longer able to do so. A power of attorney is a person you trust to act on your behalf before your death. She may or may not be the executor of your estate who handles matters after your death.

When an aging parent needs assistance paying bills and balancing the checkbook, for example, someone who has a power of attorney can do this. She can sign legal documents in your name and conduct matters on your behalf.

A note of caution also should be made here. In some cases, the person who becomes power of attorney may abuse that position. If that is the case, their power of attorney may be revoked by the aging parent if financial abuse is suspected. If the aging parent is incapacitated at the time, those concerned may need to seek guardianship or conservatorship.

Questions to consider with your parent:

- With whom do you trust to make financial decisions if you are not able to do so?
- Does he know of your decision?
- Do my siblings know of your choice? Why or why not?
- Have you specified this decision in any legal document?

F. Guardianship/Conservatorship

In order to provide appropriate care for your aging parent, sometimes the court has to step in and make decisions if no one has been designated as legal power of attorney or medical power or attorney. Jacqueline, an attorney in Connecticut says, "When a parent has dementia sometimes they really are unable to take care of their finances and they're unable to make sane medical decisions for themselves. If it gets to the point where the elderly parent is making decisions which really are not in their best interest, then you're looking at possibly getting a conservator/guardian appointed by the state for that person. That means making an application to the probate court for the child to become conservator for his/her parent." This is a last resort Jacqueline says because, "You're taking away the rights of the person who is under conservatorship." (Most states call that person a guardian. Connecticut is the only state which uses the term conservator.)

Since adults in this stage of their care are vulnerable, the court has safeguards in place to prevent possible abuse. Jacqueline says, "You're going into the court and everything is essentially protected because the conservator has to take out a bond. So if somebody is trying to get a conservator appointed for a parent, it's usually for legitimate reasons and they're subject to the oversight of the court."

G. Medical Information Sheet

This sheet is not a legal document, but should be kept and shared with medical professionals so care is not delayed or complicated because medical records are not on file. Information should include:

Date
NAME

Address, telephone no.

Next-of-of-kin/contacts: [name, relationship, telephone no. etc.]
[Name] has living will and health-care proxy [if applicable]
Name of Health Care Proxy with tel. numbers

ALLERGIC TO [Describe here any allergies, sensitivities, etc.]

Current Daily Drug Regime (include all vitamins, supplements)

TIME	DRUG	STRENGTH	DOSAGE	TREATMENT FOR:
Breakfast [examples]	XXXX	25/100	[no. of pills]	For Parkinson's
Lunch	XXXX	25/100		
Dinner	XXXX	25/100		
Bedtime	XXXX	25/100		

Medical problems: [e.g. Parkinson's disease. Diagnosed/date.; list other medical conditions/surgeries here with dates]

DOCTORS: primary care and specialists
Address, and telephone

Questions to consider with your parent:

- Is there anything you need us, as your grown children, to know about your care that we don't already know?
- Does someone know where your advanced care directives, last will and testament, and other documents are kept? (Safety deposit box, safe, drawer, file cabinet)
- What other documents are there as well?

Healthcare Concerns...Being Your Parent's Patient Advocate

It's difficult for many people to hear that someone they love is sick. It gets even more complicated when it's your parent, especially if "invisible conversations" exist in your relationship. There can be many obstacles to communicating when the stress of illness is introduced.

Abraham, who deals with a chronic condition, explains the plight of many who suffer from physical and mental illness. "It's hard to explain to someone who has no clue. It's a daily struggle being in pain or feeling sick on the inside while you look fine on the outside...never judge what you don't understand." And so, adult children, spouses or partners, friends, and other caregivers are called to be compassionate with their loved ones in the face of the unknown future while getting as much information so informed decisions can be made.

People deal differently with illness and their treatment. It's important to honor their wishes, while providing care and support in a safe manner.

❊ ❊ ❊ ❊ ❊

When my father was diagnosed with cancer, he didn't want anyone outside our family to know. He felt if people knew he was sick, it would be the end of his successful business career. So, he sought treatment five states away, living in a hotel during his chemotherapy and radiation treatments. His wife went and visited on weekends, but for the most part, he was alone. That decision was hard for me to understand, but that's what he wanted.

❊ ❊ ❊ ❊ ❊

There are numerous diseases and conditions which affect the lives of older adults...too many to mention in this text. But as I interviewed people for this book, there seemed to be much concern and fear over those diseases which affect the mind.

Alzheimer's disease and Dementia

As people age, many notice periods of forgetfulness and may worry about what is ahead for them. Many fear that forgetfulness may be a precursor to Alzheimer's disease. However, not everyone who has memory loss has Alzheimer's disease. According to the Alzheimer's Association, "Most of us eventually notice some slowed thinking and problems remembering certain things. However, serious memory loss, confusion, and other major changes in the way our minds work are not a typical part of aging." Dementia is the umbrella term which covers many forms of memory loss. Alzheimer's disease accounts for 50-70% of those cases of dementia. In 2010, The Alzheimer's Association estimated 5.3 million people in the United State had the Alzheimer's disease. They expect that number to reach 16 million by 2050.

What's the difference in typical age-related mental changes and signs of Alzheimer's and dementia?

Signs of Alzheimer's/dementia	Typical age-related changes
*Poor judgment and decision making	*Making a bad decision once in a while
*Inability to manage a budget	*Missing a monthly payment
*Losing track of the date or the season	*Forgetting which day it is and remembering later
*Difficulty having a conversation	*Sometimes forgetting which word to use
*Misplacing things and being unable to retrace steps to find them	*Losing things from time to time

(*Basics of Alzheimer's Disease*, Alzheimer's Association 2010, used with permission)

There are seven stages of Alzheimer's disease. Because the symptoms in the early stages may be confused with the normal effects of aging, many may not seek help until later stages. While there is no current cure for Alzheimer's disease, there is medical treatment to help the symptoms during the early stages. A visit to the neurologist will help to answer many questions you may have about what is happening in the life of your loved one and what to expect in the future.

Movies, such as "The Notebook," have tried to bring to light the tremendous difficulty Alzheimer's disease can bring not only to those with the disease, but to family members as well. Some say, however, the effects of the disease are more challenging than they ever dreamed.

❊   ❊   ❊   ❊   ❊

Jenny says her fear over her mother's Alzheimer's diagnosis coupled with her father's denial over her illness required her to be very frank with him. "The first conversation I had was, 'You have to go to an attorney. Mommy has Alzheimer's. And he said, 'Bull****' and I said, 'No bull***. I took her to the neurologist.' He said, 'I don't believe it.' 'He had a lot of denial, a lot of denial.' I said, 'She's going to need a nursing home.' He said, 'I'm not doing that.'" Jenny says, "I literally had to take him by the hand and have the lawyer explain it to him, and at that point he believed all of it. It took me not sitting back. I was not forceful, but I was pretty insistent. I was afraid I was going to get stuck with it all. I didn't know what was going to happen."

❊   ❊   ❊   ❊   ❊

When faced with any diagnosis, getting as much information as you can, obtaining early intervention, making good choices regarding care, and a maintaining a solid support system for yourself will give you resources to continue with compassion in the difficult days ahead.

Being a Health Care Advocate for Your Parent

Receiving medical news from a health care professional can be traumatic and confusing. It is extremely difficult to take in information about test results, diagnoses, treatment options, and aftercare if you're dealing with the emotional fallout from what you've just heard. That's why many people choose a spouse, family member, or trusted friend to be a patient advocate. Others choose to hire a professional for this role. The role of a health care advocate is different from the role of a health care/medical power of attorney. This person is someone who is an extra set of eyes and ears in the exam room, doctor's office, or hospital room. They can ask questions and make sure that your parent is receiving the information she needs and can help explain the options presented. Many interactions with health care professionals are routine and don't require an advocate, but having one at the right time can be invaluable and relieve unnecessary stress.

Pam is a single woman whose family lived in another state. She asked her friend, Sherry, to accompany her to her doctor's office when she had an appointment to discuss her upcoming kidney cancer operation and her following course of treatment. Pam asked Sherry to bring a pen and pad of paper to take detailed notes of what the doctor said and to ask any questions which she missed. Pam knew that she would be dealing with the information on an emotional level, while her friend could be more objective. Sherry says, "Just driving the hour to get there and then walking down the hallway of the prominent cancer hospital was intimidating enough, but then to have to face an expert to talk about your cancer...that would be too much for a person to do alone, much less to have any memory of what was said. I was able to ask the doctor questions which didn't come to Pam's mind and to ask them more bluntly than she could, because it wasn't about me. The doctor was very willing to answer all of our questions, and in the end I feel we got more information. Of course, all of it was written down for her to reference later."

The old saying, "Knowledge is Power" is true. While medical professionals are very willing to give information regarding their care, having a health care advocate help you ask the questions you need to make the right decisions will get you the best care.

What to consider when choosing a patient/healthcare advocate:
- Do you trust this person?
- Is this person calm when facing emotional information?
- Can this person state questions clearly?

- Does this person have issues with authority figures (i.e. will she ask what needs to be asked to a person in authority)?
- Can this person be there to comfort you/the patient if needed?
- What are this person's feelings about hospitals?
- Does this person know the patient's healthcare history enough to ask the questions which need to be asked?
- Is this person aware of your deepest concerns regarding the diagnosis, procedure, or operation?
- Does this person know what your current medications are and what allergies you have?

What the advocate/patient needs to do before the medical appointment:

- Gather all of the information he will need to give the doctor: current medications and dosages, his health history and that of blood relatives, prior surgeries.
- Discuss what his concerns are for this visit.
- Discuss what he wants you to ask and what he feels comfortable asking himself.
- If the other spouse is not going, what are her concerns as well?

Questions to ask the doctor as a patient advocate:

A. When receiving a diagnosis

- Would you clarify any of the words which are unclear?
- How did you come to this conclusion?
- What can we expect going forward?
- What is her short-term, long-term prognosis?
- What is the timeframe of progression/remission?
- Is there more than one disease which could be affecting his condition?
- What tests will you perform?
- If the tests are positive, what is the next step?
- If the tests are negative, what's the next step?
- How and when will she get the results?
- How will this affect his functioning physically, mentally, emotionally, sexually?
- What are the different treatment options and what are the risks involved with each?
- What alternative therapies have been used with this diagnosis?
- What if he decides not to have treatment?
- Which hospital is the best for this procedure/treatment and do you have privileges there?
- What medications will be required before and after this procedure or operation?
- How will these new medications interact with his existing medications?
- What are the side effects of this procedure/ medication/ illness?
- If her symptoms worsen at home, what can she do on her own first?

- When should she call you?
- If hospitalization is needed at some point, how will we know?
- When do we need to call an ambulance?
- Are there any websites or brochures you can give us for additional information?
- May I have several patient referrals?

B. When facing a procedure

- What is this test for?
- Who are the team members who will be working on him?
- How many times have they done this procedure?
- Is this procedure covered by insurance?
- Is this facility covered by his insurance?
- Will aftercare be needed at a rehab or at home with an aide?
- Is that covered by insurance?
- Are there any insurance requirements/permissions needed?
- What papers need to be filed?
- What medications will be required before and after this procedure or operation?
- What are the side effects of this procedure/ medication/ illness?
- How long before things are back to normal/what can he expect life to be like after this?
- How much pain will he encounter?
- Is there anything which he can/can't do now to prepare? (Ex: Diet, exercise, sex, medications)
- How will this affect his functioning physically, mentally, emotionally, sexually?
- Are there any websites or brochures you can give us for additional information?

C. Additional questions to consider:

- Does the doctor have the contact information for your parent's medical power of attorney and other family members?
- Does the doctor/healthcare facility have a copy of his DNR and living will?
- Do you need a second opinion? (Note: Patients of all ages sometimes don't ask questions or request a second opinion because they don't want to hurt their doctor's feelings or fear that in doing so it may affect their relationship in a negative way. However, insurance companies oftentimes want a second opinion and will support your doing so. Having more information is better than less information when you're dealing with healthcare decisions and can reinforce your choice for or against a certain course of treatment and outcome.)

There are multiple websites which give you questions to ask for specific diagnoses. For example, The Susan G. Komen Foundation has over a dozen different cards to download with questions you can ask your healthcare provider about various aspects of breast cancer and treatment options (see http://ww5.komen.org.).

Where to Live?

Planning for your future involves knowing where you will live both now and when you are nearing the end of life. The choices are different based on your financial resources. The stressed economy is affecting the costs of long-term care, along with everything else.

A MetLife report in October 2011 says, *U.S. long-term health-care costs rose as much as 5.6 percent this year, led by assisted-living expenses and are climbing at a steeper rate during a weak economy. The average cost for assisted living rose 5.6 percent to $41,724 a year, compared with a 5.2 percent increase last year. The rate for a private nursing-home room increased 4.4 percent to $87,235 a year and adult day services climbed 4.5 percent to $70 a day. Home health-aide service was unchanged at $21 an hour.*

Some people want and are able to stay in their homes with caregiving provided by family members. For others, the choice is made for them when they get ill and loved ones cannot physically manage the level of care required, or resources for full-time care at home are not available. The timing for that choice may come sooner than later due to an unexpected downturn in health. If you are an adult child caring for your aging parents, having the discussion about the range of choices is important to have sooner rather than later, giving your parent as much time to prepare and as much input as possible. Larry Blaker works with families as they make these long-term transitions. He says, "If we wait for a fall, stroke, or heart attack to happen, then we are running in a rat race."

Still, transitions at this time of life can be disruptive and disorienting. Even if plans have been discussed together, and the process has been handled with dignity and respect, there can still be deep feelings.

❀ ❀ ❀ ❀ ❀

Shirley says her mother, a widow for 27 years, knew she would eventually move into an assisted living facility. They talked about it and looked at places over a long period of time. Still, when it came time to actually make the move, Shirley says her mother was surprised. She says her mother tells others, "I was catapulted here."

This transition can be especially difficult if you're managing these decisions from a distance.

❀ ❀ ❀ ❀ ❀

After Wendy's father died, they sold the family home and moved her mother into a smaller home. But after Wendy got a call from local police saying they found her mother wandering in the neighborhood, she knew it was time for a different level of care, especially since she lived three hours away from her mother. "It's easy when you don't live nearby to not pay close attention." A social worker at the hospital where her mom was sent after that incident alerted her that something was going on with her mother neurologically. So she made the decision to move her into an assisted living facility. Wendy says, "She (her mother) hated the thought of going and became very angry at me." But at the same time, Wendy says she knew her limits. "I knew I could not care for her on several levels." Knowing her mother had regular visitors, including another aunt who lived locally, gave Wendy some comfort in her decision. She also made the three hour trip to visit several times a month. Even though Wendy had to endure her mother's comments such as, "I used to have a daughter who loved me," she says she knew her mother was in an excellent facility.

❀ ❀ ❀ ❀ ❀

Alice also lived hours away from her mother. As an only child, she too was faced with how to best care for her mother with whom she had had a long-term difficult relationship. She made the hours-long trip regularly from the northeast down to Florida over a long period of time. But Alice saw her mother wasn't thriving. Alice's daughter had an especially close relationship with her grandmother. When Alice asked her mother if she would like to be moved to a facility in the mid-west where her daughter and grandson lived, Alice's mother jumped at the opportunity.

❀ ❀ ❀ ❀ ❀

The goal of most homecare providers is to safely keep seniors in their own homes, maintaining the highest quality of life possible. For some that means having an unlicensed companion come and do light housework, cook meals, or provide non-hands on care. Licensed caregivers through an agency can provide medical care, maintain hygiene, and are usually supervised by a nurse.

❀ ❀ ❀ ❀ ❀

The year before I went to graduate school, I was hired to be a companion to a woman in my church who was in the early stages of Alzheimer's disease. Her nephew lived two hours away. "Mrs. T," as we called her, had been a recluse for the previous six months before my arrival, and my job was to get her back into her social circles as much as possible and do daily tasks with her. It was clear that this was the best decision for her and her family as she had much attachment to her home, which had been in her family for years. Over time, an overnight companion was also added. Mrs. T lived the rest of her days happily at home.

❀ ❀ ❀ ❀ ❀

Here are questions to consider which may help keep these conversations visible.

Initial observations before a conversation:

- Is this home a safe place for her/him?
- What does the house look like?
- Is there any access to the house without stairs?
- Is the person safe with a gas stove?
- Is there anyone checking in on her on a regular basis?
- Can he walk up stairs?
- Can she do all of the practical things in her life, such as take medications, keep appointments, etc…?
- If both parents are living, do both need the same level of care?

Questions to ask aging parents who are autonomous and able to make decisions:

- As you look ahead, what do you want to be doing and how can we help make that happen?
- Do you think you'd like to stay in your home or do you want to move to an assisted living facility or community?
- If we make that decision (for you to move), what does that look like and what's the timetable?
- Down the road, if and when you need additional care, would you want to be in a facility?
- Is it time to get long-term care coverage (if financially feasible)?
- What would make it possible for you to be more active and social both now and down the road?

Making the decision:

- What would your preference be?
- What is most important for you in this process?
- What can you afford? What assets do you have to cover the costs?
- Do you have long-term health care insurance?
- (If both parents being considered in this decision) do you want to be together?
- How can we make that happen?

Questions when choosing to stay at home:

- What does it mean to you to stay at home?
- Are there changes which need to be made to your home to make it accessible for you? (For example: doors widened, bathrooms/toilets enlarged, bedroom on one floor, ramps)
- Your safety and care is my top concern. How can we be sure you will be safe here?
- Do we need to get some help with meals, cleaning, dispensing of medication, or medical care?
- How much visiting do you want from family and from friends?

- How can we make sure your social needs are met?
- How will we know if this option is no longer working?
- If you have to leave, what will you want to have happen to your home?

Questions to consider when looking for a long term care facility:

- What are the different options for living spaces?
- What are the degrees of medical care in each option?
- Is there an option to own or rent?
- What is the cost of each option?
- What exactly does each option cover?
- Over what period of time is the coverage?
- If you have received quotes from different assisted living centers or nursing homes, what does the facility provide for the money?
- What are the hidden costs?
- Is there a deposit required?
- Is the facility financially secure (to ensure your parent's investment isn't lost)?
- Have you had someone review the facility's financial documents?
- How much of your parents' belongings are allowed in the space?
- How much privacy is there?
- What is the facility's stance on sexual activity among residents?
- Are there safeguards to protect your parent if she is vulnerable?
- If your parents are in different living spaces at the facility, how are visits arranged?
- What kind of social opportunities are available?
- Are there opportunities for residents who are able to volunteer?
- Does your parent need Wi-Fi? And is it available?
- Is the facility child-friendly if grandchildren come to visit?
- Does the facility allow pets (if applicable)?
- What is the demeanor of the staff?
- Do they treat the residents with respect?

Money

For Living Now

As adults begin to transition from earning years to retirement, discussions need to take place, and decisions need to be made about how they will finance the remaining years of their lives. Some may be able to do this on their own or with the help of their financial professionals. Larry Blaker works with families considering making the transition to long term care facilities. He says, in some cases the role adult children can play is often welcome. "Parents are more than happy to have someone circle the wagons with them."

Some older adults may need help gathering financial statements including annuities, pensions, IRA's, bonds, dividends, social security, and veterans' benefits, among other sources of income. For other seniors, sources of income may be limited, and aging parents may need assistance with filing for Medicaid. Some Elder Law attorneys help navigate what is called "spending down assets" so they qualify for benefits. Other attorneys caution against this practice. When considering your own family's needs, it's best to check with your attorney and financial advisor.

Letting Go of Control

It can be difficult to let go of control of your finances, especially if you have been in charge of them during your lifetime. Even if you trust the person you've chosen to manage them for you, turning over control is sometimes seen as a symbol that you're no longer independent.

❋ ❋ ❋ ❋ ❋

Jacqueline says she often sees this dynamic in her law practice. "Often you have elderly people who are beginning to lose their memory. They may have documents in place. They may have a revocable trust which may be funded. And yet as people get dementia, they're often reluctant to give up control of any kind, because they're beginning to feel vulnerable. Yet it's really time to put their assets into a trust so that the trustees they've named can begin to take over."

Jacqueline tells the story of an 80-year old client whose husband died two years ago. "Since he died, she has really begun to lose her memory both short-term and long-term. The children are trying to get her to fund her trust, to let them help her pay her bills and she's very resistant. She doesn't want to talk to them about it. She doesn't want to talk to me (her attorney) about it. She doesn't want to talk to her accountant about it or her financial advisor." Jacqueline says the family is distressed to see her not being able to take care of herself and may seek a guardianship/conservatorship which would allow them to step in, pay her bills and seek medical treatment on her behalf.

✽   ✽   ✽   ✽   ✽

Nancy says the adult children's role is a difficult one, even if you have a power of attorney. "You need to review your parent's finances and legal documents periodically. Nancy's father has recently begun dating a much younger woman, whom she suspects is taking advantage of her him. Nancy says, "Next week I plan on bringing him to the bank and explaining that it's in his best interest to have a double signature on his account, since he has been writing large checks out to his lady friend and allowing her to run up the Am Ex. With a double signature he will need my consent to write checks over $250. Hopefully he will go along with this and it will stop the bleeding. I keep talking about his friends that have walked down this path of having a second or third wife that has not ended well and them being fleeced of all they worked for."

✽   ✽   ✽   ✽   ✽

Struggles

Money can be seen as a powerful symbol of so much not only in life but also in death. It can be viewed as a generous gift and it can also be viewed as a weapon, depending on the relationship and the expectations of the surviving children. When parents look to pass on their assets to the next generations, sometimes adult children may perceive the amount as a symbol of their parent's love or lack of love during their lifetime. In many cases, feelings about money can bring conflict among families at this stage of life.

As an Elder Law attorney, Anthony Enea, says "I have all too commonly witnessed siblings, family members, and friends battle for control of the finances and care of their aging parents and loved ones. While the litigation may be for the authority to make day-to-day financial and health care decisions, sadly, the root cause is oftentimes inheritance and monetary control."

Enea says this dynamic is only the beginning of what is to come. "It is anticipated that controversies and court fights involving aging parents will rapidly grow in direct proportion to the aging U.S. population. The largest transfer of inter-generational wealth, estimated to be approximately 10 trillion dollars, will be transferred from the World War II generation to the 'baby boomers.' Unfortunately, the victim in these controversies is often the family unit. I have seen firsthand the bitterness, resentment, and destruction of relationships. The effect is best described as a 'family divorce,' the impact of which may be felt for generations."

Larry Blaker agrees. He says he often sees dysfunction, resentment, and anger between children and vulnerable or aging adults when decisions are being made about the use of assets for care. "The more there is to sell, the more vicious they become."

In over 20 years of ordained ministry, I have talked with older adults with substantial assets who have sadly said, "My kids are just waiting for me to die so they can get my money." Whether that's true in the minds of the adult children or merely perceived by the aging parent, it's extremely sad to see and experience. Sometimes those feelings may have been felt because of the family history of conversations around money, or due to the fact that the adult children haven't visited as often as the aging parent would like. Regardless of the reason, in these cases the parent is left with a perception of betrayal by the ones whom they love.

The 2007 movie, "The Ultimate Gift," based on Jim Stovall's best-selling book is a great example of the pain of this conflict. One of the early scenes is the reading of the last will and testament of billionaire patriarch "Red" Stevens. All of Red's adult children are arguing over who will get which assets and are surprised to see his video-taped message for each of them. While it's clear that Red hasn't been a saint in his life, the children are portrayed as greedily awaiting their "due." Grandson, Jason (Drew Fuller), a trust-fund baby, receives the most unusual inheritance: twelve tasks, which Red calls "gifts." Calling Jason his "last hope", Red explains these "gifts" are not related to a monetary reward but are his way of passing on what it means to be a responsible adult.

Asking the Questions Now

If possible, having open conversations about money with your aging parents before their deaths may help relieve some conflict among siblings after their deaths. If you're having difficulty, an attorney or financial planner may be able to help.

Jacqueline, an attorney, says she works with her aging clients to be open with their heirs about their inheritances while they are still mentally able. She says, "I think a lot of parents, 50% of the people we see, do not want their children to see their estate planning documents. The other 50% want their children to see them and even may send them copies, or may want one child to see them and not the others. But often parents want to keep those things private until their death for various reasons." For example, she says, "Parents often perceive that their children may have made a bad marriage and they may not even have talked to the child about that but for whatever reason, they don't trust the spouse and feel that they may be on track for divorce. In that case, it makes some sense to leave things in trust for the child to protect them in case of a divorce situation." But, she says, "If everything's being divided equally among children and the parents have a good relationship with them, then I often try and encourage people to engage in that conversation with the children about what they're planning." She says that way, "the children don't have a nasty surprise or find out that everything is left in trust for them when they expected it to be left for them outright."

Sometimes adult children are reluctant to have conversations about money with their aging parents because they're afraid of being perceived as only interested in their money. That was Jimmy's situation.

❈ ❈ ❈ ❈ ❈

Jimmy says he wishes he had talked with his mother about her finances before she died, but he didn't because he feared she would think, "All he's caring about is money." His mother, Maria, had beaten breast cancer in the past, and he was optimistic about her health, even though he knew the prognosis wasn't good after the cancer returned. Jimmy's mother had always handled the family finances. His father "didn't want to know anything" about it and put it all in her care. After Maria's death, Jimmy found out the impact of his family's invisible conversations about money. He says he wishes he had asked about his parents about their financial situation. After her death, the reality came clearer. "I didn't know how we were going to pay for things." Jimmy says his father didn't know where any of the documents were. His mother left no will, although she had a pension from the police department where she had worked for many years. Later, when Jimmy did go through all of her things, he found a sizeable check which had been written to him before her death. But when he inquired about it at the bank, he found that the account had been closed. "We don't know where the money ($90,000) went." Now he says, "I tell others, you better ask every question under the sun, because you don't want to have a blank stare when others ask you questions."

❈ ❈ ❈ ❈ ❈

Questions to consider:

- Does your aging parent trust you with financial decisions?
- If no, is there another family member designated to handle matters?
- Do you know what assets your parents have?
- Do your parents know what they have?
- Is there a third party or a group of advisors who is managing their finances?
- If no one has been designated, who should be empowered to serve as an external advisor or decision-maker (e.g., family, friends, trustee)?
- Do your siblings agree with this choice?
- Do your parents have a last will and testament?
- Who is their executor/personal representative?
- What are your parents' feelings about money?
- Do they talk about money freely?
- How will long-term care be paid for?
- How will funeral expenses be paid for?
- How will your other parent be cared for financially after this parent dies?
- Are your parents in the position to fund a revocable trust?

Try this: (from Larry Blaker of www.seniorlifeoptions.net)

Create a financial inventory for/with your aging parents

- Do they have long-term care insurance?

- Do they have stocks? Bonds? Treasury notes? Pensions? Social Security or Veteran's benefits?
- In the event that you need to liquidate assets, what is the priority?
- What are the penalties for early withdrawal or cashing in?
- What is the condition of the vulnerable adult?

If you're having trouble with the conversations, attorney Jacqueline suggests saying something such as, "Mom, I'm doing my own will and my attorney has asked what you're doing in your documents for me." This information can assist you in your own financial planning.

When Driving is No Longer Safe

Have you heard stories like these?

Margaret, who is an alert 80-year-old, was out doing errands when something went wrong. She thought she had stepped on the brake, but it was actually the accelerator. She found herself driving right into the neighborhood deli and barely missed hitting several people. She was not injured but was emotionally devastated.

At 75, Tom fainted in the store and later found out that he had 99% blockage in his arteries. His doctor told him he was lucky he hadn't been driving right then. He could have killed himself or another person.

When is driving no longer safe? There is no set guideline since people age differently, but medical professionals say as people age their ability to discern distances changes. Coming to terms with this change, however, can be difficult. The loss of the privilege to drive can be devastating to a person. It signifies a loss of freedom and independence. Remember what it was like when you first got your driver's license? You could go wherever you wanted to go, whenever you wanted to go. Facing the reality that your independence is diminishing can be extremely difficult.

The conversation about when to stop driving is invisible in some families because Mom or Dad may not want to acknowledge there is a problem. He may say people are overreacting to the recent fender benders. But for his safety and others' on the road, this is a conversation which needs to happen. And it needs to be done with dignity and respect.

❀ ❀ ❀ ❀ ❀

Shirley's mother, Marge, recently moved to an assisted living facility near her daughter after she began to show signs of dementia. Marge didn't know the area well but thought she could keep her car and learn a few routes to get around town. Shirley felt this wasn't a good idea, but they kept the car in the facility parking lot anyway. Over a period of a few weeks, they would go out together and drive around the parking lot. Marge got increasingly anxious when she couldn't find a parking spot. Shirley gently told her mother, "You're not going to be able to drive, Mom. It's not realistic." Her mother wasn't ready to admit that it was too much for her. "Maybe if I got a GPS, that would help me," Marge would say. Shirley patiently kept saying, "It's probably not going to happen, Mom. You're not going to be able to find your way around." After five months of gentle conversations, Marge stopped asking to drive.

Questions to consider with your aging parent:

- How are you feeling when you're driving?
- Have you had any accidents recently or near misses?
- I don't want anything to happen to you or anyone else. Do you think it's time you thought about not driving at night?
- What would happen if you accidently hurt someone?
- I'm concerned about your eyesight. Is it time to let someone else drive?
- How do you feel about not being able to drive?

See "Resources" section for some excellent guides on this topic.

Aging and Alcoholism

Alcoholism is often masked by other healthcare issues for people at any age, but especially in older adults. Some family members may ignore the fact that their aging loved one has either started to drink more regularly or increased her consumption over time. These are some real scenarios which illustrate when alcohol use may be an issue:

Steve always liked his cocktails. Sure he gets a little obnoxious when he drinks, but that's the way he's always been. It's really not hurting anyone and it would get him upset if anyone said anything.

Mary started drinking to ease her anxiety after her husband died. Her family doesn't realize that she is drinking more and more just to get her through the day. When they see her with a drink, they figure she needs a little something to help her through her grief and loneliness.

Jim, a 75 year old, just had a heart attack. His adult son and daughter have been noticing that their father has been more forgetful lately as well. They attributed it up to early dementia. What they don't know is that Jim has been progressively drinking more at night before bedtime.

According to The National Institute on Alcohol Abuse and Alcoholism (NIAAA), part of the National Institutes of Health, older adults have a greater sensitivity and lower tolerance to alcohol as they age. Their blood alcohol level (BAC) is higher than younger people who drink the same amount. Adults age 65 and older are more likely to be depressed as a result of drinking and moderate and heavy drinkers of this age group are 16 more times likely to die of suicide than non-drinkers.

Drinking too much alcohol over a long time can:

- Lead to some kinds of cancer, liver damage, immune system disorders, and brain damage.
- Worsen some health conditions like osteoporosis, diabetes, high blood pressure, and ulcers.
- Make some medical problems hard for doctors to find and treat. For example, alcohol causes changes in the heart and blood vessels. These changes can dull pain that might be a warning sign of a heart attack.
- Cause some older people to be forgetful and confused. These symptoms could be mistaken for signs of Alzheimer's disease.

The NIAAA recommends that people who are healthy and over age 65 should have no more than seven drinks a week and no more than one drink on any one day. One drink is equal to one of the following:

- One 12ounce can or bottle of regular beer, ale, or wine cooler
- One 8 or 9ounce can or bottle of malt liquor
- One 5 ounce glass of red or white wine
- One 1.5 ounce shot glass of hard liquor (spirits) like gin, vodka, or whiskey. The label on the bottle will say 80 proof or less.

source: http://www.nia.nih.gov/HealthInformation/Publications/alcohol.htm

Not everyone who drinks has a problem with alcohol and not everyone who has a problem with alcohol drinks more. Oftentimes issues relating to alcohol abuse are masked by other illnesses and issues with aging. The best thing to do if you think there is a problem is to talk to your parent's doctor.

If you think there may be a problem, here are some questions for reflection before you talk together:

- What makes you think your loved one may have a problem with alcohol?
- Does she have a history with alcohol use?
- Does your aging loved one appear to be drinking more than usual?
- Have you noticed different behaviors?
- Does she lie about drinking or hide the amount from you or other caregivers?
- Is there anyone who is supplying alcohol to him other than those responsible for his care?
- Does alcoholism run in the family?
- Has she had more recent falls recently? (The NIAAA says hip fractures represent the interaction between drinking and higher risks for osteoporosis)

Questions to consider asking your aging parent:

- Do you think you have a problem with alcohol?
- When you start drinking, are you able to stop?
- Have you experienced any physical injury as a result of drinking?
- Are you aware that alcohol may affect the medications you are taking?
- Do you know that alcohol is a depressant and may be making you feel worse?
- What would you think about cutting back on the amount of alcohol you drink?
- Do you understand that alcohol may be affecting your health?
- Do you ever drive after you've had a drink during the day?
- How are you getting your alcohol supply?
- Does your doctor know about how much alcohol you drink?
- Why are you drinking?

If you or your aging loved one needs help, here are some suggestions:

- Talk to a doctor, counselor, or social worker who deals with issues of aging and alcohol.
- Go to a 12 step group such as Alcoholics Anonymous (note: People can get sober at any age. I know a woman who began sobriety at age 85 and lived the rest of her life with great joy!).
- If you are a family member, Al-Anon can be a great help and support system.

When Mom or Dad is Dating

Talking to Mom or Dad about dating? Ugh. No way. If the very thought of talking to Dad after discovering he is dating a long-time family friend following your mom's death gives you the creeps, you're not alone. Caregiverstress.com says, "Nearly half (47 percent) of adult children are 'not very' or 'not at all' comfortable speaking to their moms or dads about their parents' romantic lives."

Difficulty with this conversation can be especially real if your parents had a long and happy life together. As an adult child, you may feel your surviving parent is betraying the memory of your deceased parent. Or, you may suddenly see a new side of your parent which feels very uncomfortable. Who knew women would consider Dad sexy? It may be time to bring the "invisible conversation" out into the open, otherwise, it could bring potential struggle and discord in your relationship.

❋ ❋ ❋ ❋ ❋

My father and uncle were very anxious when they learned my grandfather was seriously considering marrying a woman he had met in his assisted living facility. My grandmother had died a few years before after having over 60 happy years with my grandfather. Granddad was a real catch in my eyes....smart, mentally fit, and relatively physically healthy. But he was also lonely and talked with me about his younger "lady friend" during a visit. He told me he was aware of his sons' fears and how they were concerned he would be stuck caring for his younger 'lady friend" who was already dealing with several illnesses. I imagine my father and uncle were also somewhat concerned over his remaining finances potentially going for her medical care. In reality, my grandfather wanted companionship and probably didn't want to have to travel several floors at bedtime. In the end, my dad and uncle convinced Granddad to not make any legal commitments to his "lady friend", even though the relationship continued. One thing I give my dad credit for, at least they talked about it together.

❋ ❋ ❋ ❋ ❋

Many older adults enjoy healthy, fulfilling sex lives. Some say this is the most satisfying period of their sexual lives as they are comfortable with themselves and their partners. The melding of companionship with sexual expression is important. Sex enhancing drugs have made it easier for sexual performance to continue much later in life as well.

One concern adult children have expressed which may prompt a conversation and which may be invisible is their parent's possible exposure to sexually transmitted diseases. Most older adults in their 70's and up didn't have to deal with the plethora of STD's when they dated in their teens. Most times, they were monogamous for decades. Now, when faced with being solo, the field is wide open and so are the risks. The thought of using condoms or other protections may not have been considered.

Healthcare professionals in assisted living facilities and nursing homes have long known of the need and desire by older adults to express themselves sexually. They are also aware of the risks involved especially when an adult is vulnerable due to dementia. (Note: Be sure to check with your facility to see what safeguards are in place.)

But what if your aging parent is in a relationship with another consenting adult, either living at home or in a facility? While you may feel you need to discuss your parent's newly-ignited love life, he may not be open to it. Or, she may tell you, "It's none of your business!" It's important that you enter these conversations with respect. Everyone deserves love and companionship, no matter how old they are.

Certainly if there is an issue of elder abuse (either financially or physically), you need to have some sort of intervention in order to protect your aging parent. (See: Protecting Your Loved One).

❇ ❇ ❇ ❇ ❇

Nina suspects this may be the case with her father. "My recently 85 year old widowed father has a very attractive 59 year old female friend. She showed up at my mother's wake. I had never met her before and was very taken back. I can understand my dad was the sole care giver of my mom for the past 10 years and deserved a little attention for himself. I just did not expect a blonde bombshell my sister's age, to be his choice. I can see his attraction and it's quite obvious what she is after." Nina says she found several large checks written out to this woman in her father's bank records. "Now I need to protect my father's assets since I have POA (Power of Attorney)."

❇ ❇ ❇ ❇ ❇

Questions about dating and sex (if you dare):

- I noticed you are spending a lot of time with_____. How are things going?
- What kinds of things do you get to do together? Things you love…theater, movies, walks?
- Do you have any concerns about the relationship?
- Is she healthy and financially secure?
- I'm concerned for your safety. Are you protecting yourself sexually?

Try This:

If you are having difficulty with this area of conversation, some try approaching it indirectly. You can say something such as, "I heard about a man who was dating after his wife died and this is what happened to him……I'm wondering if you have any of those thoughts, feelings, and concerns?"

Part 3

Caregiving

Who is the caregiver?

According to one study:

❖ An estimated 65.7 million people in the U.S. have served as unpaid family caregivers to an adult or a child. About 28.5% of the respondents surveyed reported being caregivers. The percentage of people who are caregivers does not appear to have changed significantly since 2004.

❖ Caregivers have been in their role for an average of 4.6 years, with three in ten having given care to their loved one for five years or more (31%).

❖ The typical recipient of care is also female (62%) and averages 61 years of age.

❖ Seven in ten caregivers take care of someone 50 years of age or older (other categories include children with disabilities)

❖ When caregivers are asked what they perceive to be the main reason their recipient needs care, the top two problems they report are old age (12%) and Alzheimer's or dementia(10%). Other frequent mentions are mental/emotional illness (7%), cancer (7%), heart disease (5%), and stroke (5%).

❖ Long-term physical conditions are present in seven out of ten caregiving situations (69%)

❖ On average, caregivers spend 20.4 hours per week providing care.

❖ Caregivers are predominantly female (66%). They are 48 years of age, on average. One third take care of two or more people (34%). A large majority of caregivers provide care for a relative (86%), with over one-third taking care of a parent (36%). One in seven care for their own child (14%).

❖ How is caregivers' time spent? A majority of caregivers help their loved one with at least one Activity of Daily Living (ADL) (56%). The most common of these is helping the care recipient get in and out of beds and chairs (40%). Personal care tasks are also fairly common—32% help their care recipient get dressed, 26% assist with bathing or showering, 24% help with getting to and from the toilet, and 18% help deal within continence. One in five help feed their loved one (19%).

❖ Caregivers of adults help on average with 4.4 out of seven Instrumental Activities of Daily Living (IADLs), including transportation (83%), housework (75%), grocery shopping (75%), meal preparation (65%), managing finances (64%), and arranging or supervising outside services (34%). Other types of supportive activities carried out by caregivers of adults include advocating for their care recipient with care providers, government agencies, or schools (52%), and performing medical therapies or treatments (22%).

❖ Most caregivers—among those whose recipient is not in a nursing home—say at least one other unpaid caregiver helps their care recipient (66%), while only 35% use paid help from aides, housekeepers, or other people paid to help their recipient.

❖ Older caregivers, those age 65 or older, are most likely to be sole unpaid caregivers, without the support of other unpaid caregivers (47% vs. 30% of younger caregivers). Co-resident caregivers are also twice as likely to be sole caregivers (49% vs. 25% living separately)

❖ Three-quarters of caregivers live either together or within twenty minutes of their care recipient (74%). Of the caregivers who do not live with their care recipient, three-quarters visit him/her at least once a week (76%).

❖ Seven in ten caregivers are non-Hispanic White (72%), 13% are African-American, and2% each are Hispanic or Asian-American.

❖ Six in ten caregivers are married (58%). More than one-third (37%) have children or grandchildren under the age of 18 in the household.

❖ Four in ten have completed college (43%), although three in ten have had a high school education or less (29%).

❖ Four in ten have less than $50,000 in household income (42%).

Source: Caregiving US All Ages Exec Summary: 2009

Adult Children as Caregivers

Whether you are called upon to be the primary caregiver, a part-time caregiver, or asked to make decisions regarding long-term care, many adult children find themselves in a role for which they are not prepared. In the midst of their own busy lives, which oftentimes include meeting the needs of their own children, these adult children are now in the role of caring for a parent who may be increasingly dependent. Feeling caught in the middle, many are left with mixed emotions.

❋   ❋   ❋   ❋   ❋

Rene is a professional caregiver. She also is recovering from the period when she was the caregiver for both of her parents who are now deceased. Back before her father was ill, and her mother was living at home with Alzheimer's disease, Rene says her dad wanted her to be in charge of her mother's care while he was still working. "He'd say, 'Do something with your mother. I don't know what to do with your mother." She would respond, "I don't know what to do with my mother!" But Rene says her dad wouldn't pay for anything. "I said, 'You HAVE to because I can't do this all the time (Rene has 2 teens, a husband, and a business).'" Eventually they hired a woman to help with some of the responsibilities. Rene says, "Mom was not a real wanderer. She had trouble dressing herself and eating. She really had trouble making any kind of food. Three days a week (at the beginning) we had someone come in and give her lunch. My father would make the breakfast for her (something hot), and get her in the chair." Rene's brother, who was having financial problems ended up moving into the house to help as well. Rene saw this as an opportunity for him to help. "I said, 'Hallelujah...you're going there.'"

As she saw her mother slipping away with Alzheimer's, Rene says she tried to engage her mother's mind. "I used to ask her all about the family, about our pictures. I had her label them. I did it with her, so I would know who was who." As far as talking directly about her Alzheimer's progression, Rene says that was more difficult. "We didn't really talk about it. It was too scary. It's different than having cancer. It frightened her to death. When you actually think it can't get worse, it gets worse."

Later after her mother was in a nursing home and in the end stages of her disease, Rene says it was hard to hear her father's anguish over her mother. "He used to call me...call me crying, 'I don't know what to do with her. I'm afraid that Alzheimer's is going to win.'"

❋   ❋   ❋   ❋   ❋

When a family has multiple siblings who could be responsible for caregiving, there are various ways of figuring out how best to care for your parent's needs. Some divide the responsibilities among the adult children. The one who is good with money takes care of paying the bills, the one who has more time on her hands takes on more of the scheduling and transporting to doctor appointments, for example. When siblings live far away from their parent, one person may be designated as the primary caregiver.

Here are two stories of how adult children have incorporated their caregiving into their lives:

✳ ✳ ✳ ✳ ✳

Shirley's mother has non-Alzheimer's dementia which has progressed fairly rapidly. Her mother was clear she didn't want to stay in the town where she had lived when her husband was alive. When talking with her siblings Shirley says, "None of them wanted her near them, so we chose the nicest place that deals with insurance (Her mother has long-term care insurance). I didn't have to fight for this one." Shirley also says her mother "knew intuitively it would be best for her to live down by me." While Shirley says that was the best decision, her mother's condition almost immediately declined drastically after her move. "It hurts to watch her like this," Shirley says. The sometimes tense dynamics of their mother-daughter relationship have also been magnified. "It hasn't been easy," Shirley says. When her mother gets cranky, she says she tries to use humor. She says she listens to her mother's complaints and validates her feelings, trying not to take her cranky moods personally. "It's important to let them know, 'You're being hard on me today' or 'You're not yourself today.'" In the end Shirley says this time of their lives together requires her to access her deepest strengths. "This is the test of how good of a person I can be."

✳ ✳ ✳ ✳ ✳

Jane, a full-time trial attorney, wife, and mother of two says the role of caregiver was thrust on her unexpectedly. When her father went into have knee surgery to improve the quality of his life, her parents didn't tell her what would be required during his aftercare. Jane says she thought it was an outpatient procedure, but in reality his care required a stint at a rehabilitation facility. Since her mother didn't drive, that meant her parents were expecting Jane to care for her mother. But that expectation was part of an "invisible conversation" until the events were put into motion. Caregiving required some quick adjustments to her family schedules. Jane soon discovered a deeper reality, however. The concentrated time together with her mother proved to be a reality check. She saw her mother's accelerating dementia first-hand and how her father had been covering it up. "I wished I had understood that they were hiding in the house...hiding some problems that I should have asked more questions about. I missed a lot of opportunities. But thank God I found out before it became dangerous."

Jane says the journey with her mother through her decline required much attention.

"Sometimes it's not conversations, it's observation...It's hard to have conversations with people about why they can't tie their shoes...The real questions occur when ordinary

activities are too much for them or you notice (things) are not being done, like laundry. When you start to notice these changes, you need to ask, 'Do you need help?' and 'What can I do to help?'"

Jane's parents needed different facilities for their health issues. "You live a lifetime in a few years. It's been the worst year and the best year. She (Mom) has told me some great stories of when I was little (good long-term memory…no short-term memory) and how she met my dad. It's been great to be able to care for her in that way." Jane says she tries to keep it all in stride and, like others, she uses humor to diffuse potentially difficult situations. When her mother balked at some of her comments and questions about her finances, Jane said, "Hey…I'm just keeping it real like Dr. Phil!" She says she also tries to do things which are still meaningful, like making the weekly 90-minute round-trip to Biscuitville to get and deliver her parents' favorite hot biscuits to them. She tells them she's sneaking in contraband!

❋ ❋ ❋ ❋ ❋

Talking With Your Spouse and Children about Grandma and Grandpa

When you are the caregiver for your aging parent, your family's life is impacted as well. Family members may be called upon to help with caregiving activities or they may have to take on additional responsibilities around the house when you are with Mom or Dad.

❋ ❋ ❋ ❋ ❋

Rene has two teenage sons and says, "It cut into their whole lives. Someone has been sick for the majority of their growing up." At the beginning, Rene was honest with them and told them straight out, "Grandma has Alzheimer's." The impact on both boys was deep. They tried to spend all the holidays together with her until her mom wasn't able to any more. When her father was ill and at the end of life, her older son went to visit him regularly and was able to have the conversations he needed to have with him before he died.

❋ ❋ ❋ ❋ ❋

Many say encouraging family members to be open and honest about the impact of caregiving on their families has been important. They say they may have avoided potential invisible conversations by letting each person give in to their aging loved one in a way which feels most comfortable while honoring their limits when they feel they can't give more.

❋ ❋ ❋ ❋ ❋

Shirley, whose mother has dementia, says her teens have had differing reactions to her mother's needs. Shirley's daughter is not able to do much on her own without others there to help. Her son, however, still takes his grandmother out on shopping trips. Shirley says after becoming exhausted during a 6-hour venture one time, he's now clearer about how much he can handle. They have now also hired someone to assist them in taking Shirley's mother out on day trips, which they know she needs and loves.

❊ ❊ ❊ ❊ ❊

Questions to ask yourself as you begin/consider caregiving responsibilities:

- What will it look like going forward for my parent, for me, for my family?
- How sick will they get?
- Are you interested in being a part of this process or in helping in any way?
- If yes, what can you do? Sit with them to visit, read or be there while the caregiver takes time away, prepare light meals, take her shopping (if so, what are the logistics?)
- How long are you willing to give?
- Will you know whom to call if you have a problem/emergency?
- What is this responsibility going to entail?
- Are there needs for overnight caregiving?
- Who will take that responsibility?
- What are my own limits?
- What can you do?
- What are you willing to do?
- What will you do if into the process you realize that it's too overwhelming?
- How will you support yourself while you're in this process?
- Does your company give eldercare benefits?
- If yes, what are the parameters? Whom do you need to notify?
- Are you concerned about utilizing eldercare benefits?
- Is there a potential cost to you or repercussions for your job?
- What are the benefits of your caregiving role to you and your loved one?

Invisible Conversations with Outside Caregivers

I f you've ever been a patient in the hospital or in other any place which requires you to depend on the care of others, you know it can be a jolt to your sense of independence. It's no different for many older adults who may now have to rely on others as a permanent way of life. People who have been autonomous for decades are now vulnerable as they depend on others for simple tasks. So, choosing the right person to give care to your aging parent is crucial not only for your parent's peace of mind, but yours as well.

Fortunately there are thousands of skilled and compassionate caregivers who willingly do the work that many of us can't or won't do on a daily basis. They interact with people on an extremely intimate basis every day. They may or may not be licensed. They may come from an agency or may be known to your family by referral. Being clear about the physical needs of your aging parent will help you decide what skills you need in a caregiver.

As in any relationship, "invisible conversations" can exist between caregivers and older adults. Think about it. You're bringing two people together in an intimate environment, sometimes for hours a day. They may have vastly different life experiences and cultural backgrounds. The older adult may be feeling very vulnerable due to a loss of function. And yet, these two are forging a new relationship under these circumstances. So how do you make sure that communication continues to be open with dignity and respect on both sides?

Sometimes it may be as simple as the way something is said. Here are two examples:

Betty, a 75-year-old who visits a 95-year-old friend regularly, says, "I hate it when people (caregivers) call you 'honey,' 'baby,' or 'sweetie' as a put down." Betty says it's not the words which are being said, it's the tone and energy behind it which she finds condescending.

An accomplished businessman at the end stages of cancer spent his final days in a wheelchair. He cringed every time his home health aide would say something like, "Come on, sweetie, let's get you dressed." While that comment was most likely meant in a sincere way, it sounded condescending to someone whose mind was still alert. His response was to close his eyes and pretend he was asleep.

On the other hand, caregivers may have "invisible conversations" as well. One of them involves the role of racism. Unfortunately many Caucasian older adults of all socio-economic backgrounds may still be harboring racist attitudes which may have been viewed as socially acceptable in their earlier years. Popular novels, such as _The Help_, by Kathryn Stockett, have brought to light the feelings and struggles of African American service providers during the journey toward Civil Rights in the United States. Many experienced racism at the hands of their white employers. Yet, as far as we've come as a nation, many people still hold deep racist feelings. If you are responsible for overseeing the hiring of an aide, it is important to know how your aging loved one feels about people of different races and to be clear about what behavior is and isn't acceptable.

Finding the right fit of caregiver with your aging parent may take a few tries. But once the match is made, it can be worth more than gold. In some families there is such a connection made, that the aide is embraced with great affection and seen as a family member all the way through the eventual funeral. The skill, care, and love they exhibit during life's most human experiences have earned them that status.

Questions to consider as you are looking for more help:

- How much time do you need from an aide?
- What type of responsibilities are you looking for an aide to do?
- Do you need a licensed aide vs. an unlicensed companion?
- Do you need your aide to have supervision from a nurse for potential medical issues?
- Does your insurance/Medicare cover this type of care or will you have to pay out of pocket?
- If you are paying out of pocket, who will be financially responsible and for how long?
- What plan do you have in place if the money runs out?
- What type of person will best suit your parent? Cultural background, age, gender?
- How will you know if this person is working out well with your parent?
- Will this person live in or outside the home?
- If this person has children of her own, is it OK for her to bring them in an emergency?

Questions and conversations with potential aides:

- Discuss how much time you think you will need from them.
- What are your credentials?
- Do you have references?
- How much energy and involvement do you have to be with an elderly person?
- What types of activities did you do with your last charge?
- What did you like/dislike about your last position as an aide?
- How will your own family deal with your being here (do they have responsibilities which will interfere?)
- (If your parent has pets) Do you have any allergies to pets?
- How would you handle an emergency situation?

Questions to ask your aging loved ones:

- How do you feel about having an aide come to help?
- What kinds of personality traits do we need to look for in an aide?
- How can we protect your privacy while there is someone new in your home?
- How will you let me know if she is not working out?

Communicating with Siblings

Whether you're close with your siblings or not, caregiving responsibilities can cause stress within family communications.

❀ ❀ ❀ ❀ ❀

Shirley says, "It's hard when families don't function as a unit. Even in the best interest of my mother's mental health, there's schism. In a perfect world siblings would be able to work together, be transparent. In Shirley's situation, one sister started to make decisions without consulting anyone else. Other siblings had "black holes" operating. "That's when people don't talk to each other for long periods of time. It's like they drop off the face of the earth." Shirley says keeping the dialogue going is important. "One might say, 'I disagree with you.' 'OK,' she says, 'but we still need to talk.'"

❀ ❀ ❀ ❀ ❀

Jenna is a part-time caregiver of an elderly woman who has Alzheimer's disease. The elderly woman is a former nurse and told her family that she never wanted to be in a nursing home. In order to make that possible her adult daughter, son, and daughter-in-law moved into the family home with her to help and to save money on caregiving expenses. They leased a hospital bed and made other necessary changes to her home.

But Jenna says things quickly deteriorated. "She's been through falls, breaking of ribs, hallucinations, and now she's an invalid. The son and daughter-in-law think she belongs in a nursing home and they're resentful, even though they said they would move in to help take care of her." Jenna says the tension in the house between the siblings is palpable. She says they continually try and talk to each other through her, even though they live in the same house and she's only there part-time. "They don't talk at all. The effect is RAGE. You just hope that they talk to each other at the funeral." Jenna thinks their deep anger is about who should be responsible. "Nobody wants to help. They moved into the house so they could 'help Mom with Alzheimer's'. Now she's on Medicaid, but because they live in the house, they can't get 24-hour care, they can only get eight hours of care a day." The rest of the costs for their mother's care comes out of their pockets.

❀ ❀ ❀ ❀ ❀

Jacqueline, an Estates and Trusts attorney, says money is often the cause of sibling discord. "We often find a sense of unfairness or inequity between siblings which usually can pop up while the parents are alive, but at the death of the surviving parent is really when it becomes evident. There are events which may have happened years and years ago that fester in people. Sometimes they do bring them up with their parents or their siblings but often they don't. Things as silly as: 'My brother has four children and I have two children and my parents paid for my brother's children's education which is not fair because I only have two children and he has four children.'"

Regina has worked with many families dealing with long-term illnesses and says parents can help alleviate some of the friction among their children both before and after their deaths. "When you make a trust or will or put executors in place, you need to explain why you're going one route instead of another. Even if people don't accept it or like it, at least it needs to be explained, so that after you've died there isn't talk of "Well, Mom didn't mean that," or 'Why did she do that?' If the kids don't like the reasons, at least the reasons are known and they are expressed."

These are some of the possible invisible conversations which can occur among siblings:

- He/she is not being transparent enough. I don't know what's going on.
- (About the caregiver) He is taking all of the money. I don't trust her.
- (About a non-caregiver) He is taking advantage of Dad and taking his money.
- I don't want to be involved. If I ignore this, it will go away.
- Dad wouldn't want this decision to be made.
- No one is helping me. All of the responsibility has fallen on me.
- All she cares about is Mom's money.
- Dad gave my sister money when he was alive. He promised me he would give me more after he died.

Questions to consider for conversations with siblings:

- Do you have any questions or input as to how I'm dealing with Mom or Dad?
- This is my understanding of what her wishes are. Do you have any other information?
- How can we all make sure Mom's wishes are met both now and in the future?
- How can we make sure we're communicating with each other?
- What can we each do to help in this situation to make sure Mom's needs are met? I can do…what about you? or I need help. Can you do ……?

Loss and Grief

Loss is a normal part of human life. It occurs when a person lets go of something or someone. Grief is experienced as the feelings resulting from loss. As people age, they are faced with a multitude of losses in their lives. Progressing through loss and the accompanying feelings of grief, may occur for those who are facing the last days of their lives.

✻ ✻ ✻ ✻ ✻

Maria was in her 90's when I met her as her chaplain. She was already in hospice care, which meant that she had less than six months left to live. As I visited with her over the months, I was impacted by every encounter. We talked about her journey over to the US from Italy before WWII. We talked about her love for her family, how she would miss them, and how much she knew they would miss her. We talked about her unshakeable faith which allowed her to embrace those last days with great courage. And we talked about what she expected would happen after her death.

✻ ✻ ✻ ✻ ✻

But, loss begins for people long before death occurs and needs to be recognized. Aging often includes the downsizing of a life which may have once included many elements. This transition may include the loss of: physical surroundings when someone moves from a house to an apartment, an assisted living facility, or a nursing home; family relationships, as spouses or partners die and adult children move away; friendships as peers begin to die or move away to facilities; independence or mobility as driving abilities may end, and physical ability wanes.

In their book, *All Our Losses All Our Griefs: Resources for Pastoral Care*, Kenneth Mitchell and Herbert Anderson outline the major forms of loss people of all ages experience. (Used with permission from the publisher: Westminster John Knox Press.)

1. Material Loss: The loss of a physical object or of familiar surroundings to which one has an important attachment.

    Older adults may experience this type of loss if they leave their home and move to a new community, for example. Their support systems including house of worship, friends, even the familiarity with their local grocer or dry cleaner are now gone.

    For families of older adults, this loss may be felt in the sale of a home which had been in the family for decades or a hometown base which was known and visited.

2. Relationship Loss: The ending of opportunities to relate oneself to, talk with, share experiences with, make love to, touch, settle issues with, fight with, and otherwise be in the emotional and/or physical presence of a particular other human being.

    This type of loss may occur for older adults when a spouse/ partner or other dies, or divorces, or if she moves away from close friends. It may also occur with changes in caregivers who have been close to her.

    For families of older adults, relationship loss may have occurred with the death of the other parent prior to the current situation. It may also be in effect with the shift in relationship with the surviving parent due to diminishing cognitive abilities.

3. Intrapsychic loss: The experience of losing an emotionally important image of oneself, losing the possibilities of 'what might have been,' abandoning plans for a particular future, the dying of a dream. Although often related to external experiences, it is itself an entirely inward experience.

    For older adults looking into the future, this loss of how they imagined their lives to be is real and deep. A long awaited trip, or even retirement, or anticipation of a big family event may not be an option now.

    For families this loss may occur as the dying of the idea that the family will no longer continue to enjoy vacations with Grandma or Grandpa due to their condition or health. If family members are the caregivers, the loss may entail the changing of lifestyles to accommodate the aging loved one.

4. Functional Loss: Powerful grief can be evoked when we lose some of the muscular or neurological functions of the body.

    An older adult may realize she is in the early stages of dementia or Alzheimer's disease and anticipate what's ahead for her. She may worry about her spouse and how he will manage when her condition progresses. Older adults may also experience this loss with the realization that they can't toilet, wash, or feed themselves anymore without the help of others.

    For families, the idea that Mom or Dad is slipping away and may not be able to remember them or their grandchildren can bring significant grief.

5. Role Loss: The loss of a specific role or of one's accustomed place in a social network.

    For older adults, having a community that keeps them active and engaged, as well as intellectually stimulated is vital. Social networks also provide places which value the services and expertise they may provide as volunteers or philanthropists. The loss of these roles signals for some they no longer have an outlet to express meaning in their lives.

With this type of loss, families may have to adjust to the idea that the man or woman who may have been "larger than life" in terms of their role in society has changed. Adult children now become the heads of the family and even perhaps take on the role of caregiver to those who once took care of them.

6. Systemic Loss: Human beings usually belong to some interactional system in which patterns of behavior develop over time; when functions in the system disappear or are not performed, the system, as a whole, as well as its individual members experience systemic loss.

Older adults might experience this type of loss as they see their family dynamic change along with their condition.

Families may feel "our family may never be the same again." Things are different without Mom or Dad around, even if they are still living.

Other Terms

During a seminary course called "Death, Dying and Grief," I was introduced to two additional terms which may be helpful: *anticipatory grief* and *complicated grief*.

Anticipatory Grief refers to the grieving which is done before an actual loss occurs. When an aging loved one dies after having Alzheimer's disease or dementia, for example, family members may have grieved for years as they watched their mother slipping away, no longer recognizing them or their children. They know the person she once was, left them long before her actual death. Mood changes with angry outbursts showed them, this was not the wife/mother/sibling/friend they once knew and loved. They are often struck with a marked sense of relief when the person dies because they know their loved one is no longer suffering.

Complicated Grief occurs when someone hasn't finished the grieving process in one situation before another loss occurs. This may happen if both parents die within a relatively short period of time. It may also occur if a person never finished grieving a loss from many years ago. Any future loss then taps back into those unresolved feelings and can create a sense of immobility.

❀ ❀ ❀ ❀ ❀

Kathy was close to her mother but did not get along with her father or her sister. Because she was busy with her own life when her mother died, she didn't fully work through all of her feelings of loss. She was surprised at how hard it was for her when her father died several years later. She wondered why she kept thinking of her mother and found herself depressed and lethargic. Her relationship with her husband suffered as well.

❀ ❀ ❀ ❀ ❀

Everyone experiences loss in life. Processing feelings of grief as a result of those losses is an important task to maintaining your emotional, physical, and spiritual health. Talking about your loss with a trusted friend, family member, or mental health professional will help you and those you love heal and move forward together.

Questions to ask yourself or to discuss with others as you face loss in your relationship with your aging loved ones:

- What changes have you seen in your loved one recently?
- What do you miss most about the way your loved one used to be?
- Do you ask yourself, "When is she going to die?"
- If so, do you feel guilty for feeling that way?
- Do you worry about how you'll manage once she dies?
- Do you find yourself wanting to pull away or get overly close for any reason?
- Are you feeling hurt, angry, or abandoned by the impending loss of your loved one?
- Are you finding yourself feeling stuck or depressed?
- How has the current care situation affected/changed your own relationships (scheduling, change in relationship, impact of feelings on the family)?
- How will the loss of this person impact your life after his death (emotionally, financially, spiritually, logistically, and physically)? Your family's life?
- Is there any sort of recognition of the past or memories that you can still share together?
- Is there anyone you need to talk to now about the role of this loss in your life?
- How are you caring for yourself in the midst of your grief?

Remembering, Before it's Too Late

Even if your parent has already begun to experience some dementia, her long term memory may still be intact. One way to care for your parent is to continue to have a sense of curiosity about her and make sure you record as much as possible of her early life experience. This can be done over time using a tape recorder or a pen and notebook.

Wendy, a writer from California, offers some good suggestions:

Wendy went through some of her father's things after his death and found a box of memories from his military service during World War II. She says she wishes she had asked more about his experiences when he was alive, but, she says things were different with that generation. "It's not that I didn't care. I just didn't ask the questions and no one I know asked them either." She says some family secrets may have kept her from asking more back then. Now, she says she would do it differently. When getting information for your family history, Wendy suggests making a distinction between questions of history and personal experience. "I want the human aspect about what it was like to go through the Alps of Italy. What did you see and feel?" versus broad information such as "How was the war?" Other specific questions might be, "What was your typical day like? What was the terrain like? What was the weather like? I can't imagine walking so far in the cold..." Comments and questions like that might trigger them to remember other things and continue to give you more information.

Wendy says, "Don't be afraid to pressure a little bit and don't give up at the slightest hesitation. But also, you don't want to cause stress, which is an enemy for many illnesses. Instead you can get back at the information another way." Wendy suggests changing the topic for a minute, telling a story and then relating it back to what you want to know. An example might go like this: I read in the paper that a local veteran just came home from serving and is having a hard time readjusting to his life here. "How was it for you when you returned? Did you have a hard time getting back to life as you knew it? Did you miss your buddies? I can't imagine having gotten so close and then all of a sudden never seeing them again."

Different illnesses may require additional creative ways to discover important information about family history you want to preserve.

Wendy's mother had Alzheimer's disease. She knew she needed to continue to get information about her family history in less direct manner than with her father. "I put it back on me." Wendy would say, "Mom, I forget what you told me about this..." or "I know you told me about Grandma. Can you refresh my mind? And do you mind if I take notes?"

Sometimes family stories can come alive when connected with family heirlooms and specific traditions.

❄ ❄ ❄ ❄ ❄

Penny's mother had always taught her daughters to value "good things." Penny grew up hearing the motto: "Buy what you can afford and what will increase in value over time." Her parents spent much of their married life buying antiques and valuables which have either monetary value or at the least sentimental value to her and her sisters. As her mom began to think about her initial downsizing move, she made up a list of all her valuable items and sent it out to her daughters asking them to designate the items which had meaning to them. She then collected the lists and made her last will and testament based on that information. Penny also began asking her mother questions and taking notes on the history of some of the family treasures as well. That way, when items were eventually passed down, she and her sisters would know the significance of what they were really getting.

❄ ❄ ❄ ❄ ❄

Nina says keeping her mother's traditions alive has been important to her family. "My mom was a wonderful homemaker. My grandma was also a wonderful cook and kin keeper. In her late years I remember calling her for a family favorite recipe and she would call me back 20 times after she gave me the recipe with ingredients she forgot to mention. When I saw my mom take a turn with her dementia, I sat her down before the next holiday and made her show me step by step and wrote everything down so I could carry on her family recipes. She is now in Heaven and I am the kin keeper with the recipe box."

Questions to parents from their adult children:

- What you would like me to know? (For example: stories about their early years that you may not know)
- How would you like to be remembered?
- What do you remember about your parents when they were growing up?
- What were the times were like then?
- How did you meet your spouse?
- Are there stories about something you did that you may think I don't know about? (These are always good ones for a laugh and/or a groan!)

Conversations for parents to have with their adult children:

- Tell them about things you did which may be surprising to your children (did you ever get into trouble or do outrageous things?)
- Tell them how you and their other parent met.

- Tell them stories about your childhood which they may or may not know.
- Tell them about career paths you never took.
- Tell them about unfulfilled dreams.
- Tell them about your early memories of them as children.

Completing the Relationship...Unfinished Business

A therapist I know once said, "It's far better to get your unfinished business taken care of before a person dies, than after they do." As hard as it may be, clearing up or coming to peace with the conflicts, misunderstandings, and judgments of the past before your parent dies can be powerful beyond words. It not only has the potential to free your parent to face death differently, it also can set you free to live your life in a whole new way. Your parent may need to say some things to you as well.

❋ ❋ ❋ ❋ ❋

*Bridget says her dad welcomed conversations at the end of his life. They were easy and visible. Since her mother had died six years earlier, they had plenty of time to talk about a lot of things. She noticed, however, that he would often refer to her troubled teen years when she was in the room with another visitor. "After telling so many people I was a terrible teenager, I thought that maybe I should make amends again (a process of taking responsibility for one's past, done in 12 step programs). I said, 'I know I was a terrible teenager with terrible drug and alcohol issues and I'm terribly sorry for that.' He said nothing. 'Maybe he needed to rest assured about that. He adored me, but every time someone came to visit, he threw me under the bus, and I said, Dad! Come on! I think he held on to some of that...what a pain in the *** I was.'"*

Bridget's father also discussed with her his concerns about her brother in his last days. She felt her brother had tried to take advantage of her father financially after moving in with him during his last years. He asked Bridget, "What are we going to do about your brother?" She asked, "Are you worried about him?" Bridget says she was very clear that she wanted to keep clear boundaries in the relationships. "I nicely said, 'Hmmm. Are you worried about me?' He said, 'Oh God, no.'" Then Bridget said to her father, "You're the only one who can address that with him."

Sometimes relationships can't be completed at the time of death.

❋ ❋ ❋ ❋ ❋

Mandy says her relationship with her mother was complicated. Mandy was in early sobriety when her mother suddenly found out she was dying of cancer and had only months to live. While her sister was able to say what she needed to their mother, Mandy wasn't ready to have that kind of conversation yet. "I was not comfortable enough in my self to be able to do it." Mandy says something deep inside told her to wait. "There was something bigger than me that was letting me know that this wasn't okay, because I wanted to push ahead, and it was never right. It was never the right time. It would have been all about me, saying whatever I needed to say however it came out regardless of another being. So, in some way I'm grateful those conversations never happened, because I think in the long run, I'd feel worse about it. Who I am today (is different)... And this is more the person I want to be."

After her mother's death, Mandy says she was able to make peace with her mother after a friend gave her a "gift" with this suggestion. He told her, "When you see other people who would have been your mother's age, do something nice for them. That has been a major way of healing." Mandy says a good friend of her mother's was alone and without family. Mandy took the 30 minute trip and spent time with her when she was sick, brought her a plant, and checked in with her from time to time. "I can do that. And that's really more of an amends to her than going to the grave because going to the grave for me would just be words."

❋ ❋ ❋ ❋ ❋

Questions to consider asking when a loved one is dying:

- Are you ready to die?
- Are you afraid?
- Is there something I can do to help you feel more ready?
- Is there something you wanted to do that you haven't been able to do that's possible for me to do for you?
- Is there anything you need to say to me or someone else in your life which has been unspoken?
- Do you have any leftover resentments or fears which need to be spoken?
- Do you need to forgive anyone for anything or ask for forgiveness from anyone?
- Do you have any regrets in your life?
- Does anyone need to hear you say something to them?
- Do those closest to you know you love them?
- How do you want to be remembered and celebrated after your death?

Try This: Take some time to reflect about completing unfinished business with the person in your life who is dying:

- If you could say anything to your dying loved one what would it be?

- What are your deepest feelings about this person?

- What are the things for which you most appreciate this person?

- What are your greatest disappointments about this person?

- Do you have any anger toward him or her?

- Is there any event in your life with this person which needs to be revisited?

- Is there anything for which you need to forgive this person?

- Is there anything for which YOU need forgiveness from this person?

- In addressing this person, what is your motivation?

- What are the risks/advantages for you to talk with them now?

- What are the risks/advantages for them in having a conversation now?

- Is there any support system you need in completing this work?

- Will there be any ramifications to the health of your loved one as a result of this conversation?

- What do you hope to accomplish in saying this now?

- Will you have any regrets for NOT saying what you need to say before he dies?

- What are you hoping will happen as a result of talking to him?

- Are you prepared to have a different outcome than what you are expecting?

- How has holding any of this conversation inside affected you through your life?

- What needs to happen for you to be able to talk? Do you need to be alone? Do you need them to be coherent?

- Do you think you will feel better or worse about yourself after this?

- If there has been a long-standing disagreement, is there anything for which you can take responsibility as you begin to talk?

Try This:

If you cannot imagine yourself having these conversations with your parent, you might try this:

- Write what you want to say on a piece of paper before you say it. You can read it aloud in front of a mirror or say it to a trusted friend or spouse to make sure you are saying what you need to say and in a way that will be most fruitful for both you and the dying person.

- Role play your conversation with someone you trust to see what feelings may come up for you in the conversation so you're not surprised. If you need help, ask a therapist, clergyperson, or friend for guidance in working through your feelings and making sure your wording is what you intend.

Remember: There's an apt slogan which says: "Say what you mean, just don't say it mean." Neither of you will feel good in the long run if you speak with hatred or blame. The point is to be truthful, to say what you haven't been able to say, and to allow both of you to move forward with more freedom. If you end up not being able to say what you need or want to say to the person's face, try saying it to a picture of him first.

In the end, don't worry. All is not lost if you aren't able to speak honestly while the person is living. You can still say whatever you need to say down the road at the grave, in a therapist's office, in a support group, or to an empty chair.

Preparation for Death

As people begin to prepare for their death, some may feel cautious about bringing up certain conversational topics, feeling they don't want to do anything to upset their aging loved one. And some conversations are, indeed, off limits. One of the things I learned while training as a hospital chaplain is the final stage of life is not a time to rearrange someone's "theological furniture." That means while some may have "deathbed conversions" no one should try and change the person's theological beliefs which have held them in life and which give them a framework of support and comfort. But conversations which are sincere and loving during this time may produce some of the most honest moments together, even if you feel a bit nervous.

❋ ❋ ❋ ❋ ❋

Naomi was raised in what she calls a "culturally Jewish" home. While they celebrated the major High Holy days, she says her mother's belief system around God was always questionable. As her mother neared death, Naomi asked her mother, "Who would you like to speak at your funeral?" She says they had always had a very open and honest relationship and Naomi assumed her mother was fully accepting of her impending death, based on their previous conversations. Naomi was shocked, she says, when her mother burst into tears. "She hadn't pictured her funeral...It hit me in a way neither one of us expected and I remember thinking, 'I wish I hadn't asked that.'" However, in another conversation, they talked more about her funeral. Since Naomi's niece is a Rabbi, her mother wanted her to preside at the service. Knowing what the elements of the service might be and about her mother's history with her faith, led her to ask, "What do you believe about God?" Naomi says they had a long discussion after that. Her mother said she felt God was "fair and just." She talked not about her life ending, but as "going on a journey" where she would see and have conversations with her husband and other loved ones who had died before her. She also talked about having seen "the light." Naomi says she was comforted by what her mother told her. "It was good for both of us to have that conversation at the end of life."

Conversations in the final days...

Many people are on heavy medication during their final days of life, in a semi-conscious or fully unconscious state. However, there may still be opportunities to have interesting interactions with your loved one.

When Naomi's mother was a day or two away from death and on heavy doses of morphine, the nurse told her, "If there's anything that you need to apologize for, now's probably the time." Naomi says she racked her brain and then approached her mother's bed whereby she confessed to having had a party at the house decades before as a teen, which her mother didn't know about. After her confession, her mother cracked open her eyes, smiled and said, "Oh Naomi!" and closed her eyes again!

A few days later one of Naomi's mother's closest friends, Lila, came to see her as well. Knowing that she had always loved Lila's homemade cookies, she brought one to her bedside. Naomi didn't want to hurt Lila's feelings and tried to figure out what to do. She took a small crumb from the cookie and rested it in between her mother's lips. ...whereby her mother opened her eyes and said, "Heaven can wait!"

❈ ❈ ❈ ❈ ❈

On a more serious note, a friend who was a hospice nurse for over three decades said she was given a card with words from an unknown author for use in helping people with their final conversations with loved ones. The card simply states:

What Can I Do To Die Healed?
Consider these statements from and to your loved ones:
Forgive Me, I Forgive You, I Love You, Thank You, Goodbye.

Questions to consider with your parent:

- How do you feel about death?
- How do you feel about the process of dying?
- Do you want to be cremated or buried? (Your religious tradition may dictate the answer)
- What do you think happens after death?
- Have your thoughts about this changed during your life?
- Do you need/want to talk to anyone (spiritual advisor) now or later?
- Do you picture your death in any particular way?
- If you could choose the scene at your death, what would it look like?
- Do you want to be alone or do you want to be surrounded by family?
- What are your desires?
- Is there anyone who needs to be here who isn't here now? (In my work, I have experienced numerous times where someone will actually wait to die until a person he needs to say goodbye to arrives. Then he is able let go and die.)

Pre-Planning for a Memorial Service or Funeral

My experience is that there are many people who would like to design or at least have input into the content of their funeral or memorial service. This can also be a real gift to the survivors who may be dealing with grief and numerous details following the death of a loved one. If many of the details are completed while your parent is still able, service planning is much easier and family members can be assured their parent's wishes have been met.

❋ ❋ ❋ ❋ ❋

I was sitting in my office one day when a man and his wife came to see me. I had never met them before, but they said that they wanted to talk about renting our church hall for an upcoming funeral service...his. He then began to tell me that he was in the end stages of cancer and wanted to plan his service as much as possible before he got to the point where he couldn't. They expected a large crowd would come and wanted to make the arrangements ahead of time so that everyone was on board.

Over the next weeks we had several conversations to iron out all of the logistics, and when the time came everyone knew what to expect and what part they would have in the service. The preparations allowed the man's wife and children to be able to grieve at his death and greet family friends at the service, rather than having to be caught up in the planning at the last minute.

❋ ❋ ❋ ❋ ❋

In another situation, a husband and wife who were very active in my congregation were both facing death from cancer. The wife had struggled for years off and on with lung cancer and was nearing the end of her life, when her husband was diagnosed with an aggressive form of brain cancer. It was heartbreaking for everyone who knew them in the church community. But it was equally as moving to see how he and his two adult daughters chose to handle this difficult time. Both daughters lived hours away but scheduled regular visits during the final months. Their father visited with me when he knew he had a few months left to live. I asked him if there was anything in particular he wanted or needed from me. He was very clear about his wishes. He told me how and when he wanted me to visit him and his wife in the days ahead. He told me specific scriptures and music which had been meaningful to them both, which he wanted to be included in their joint funeral service. He also left some details to be filled in by his daughters at a later period based on what they wanted. When it came time for the service several months later, while it as still very sad, everyone knew that the service was a true reflection of who they were as a couple.

❋ ❋ ❋ ❋ ❋

Questions to consider:

- What kind of service would you like (if you would like one at all)?
- Where would you like it to be held? (Will it be a religious or non-religious service? In some traditions, such as Christian Science, there may not be a desire to have a service or graveside burial at all.)
- What kind of mood do you want at the service? (For some this will be a celebration, for others a somber remembrance of life.)
- What scripture verses, sacred readings or secular readings would you like to include as meaningful to you?

- What music would you prefer? Are there specific hymns? Is there non-religious music which would be meaningful?
- Whom do you want to preside (which clergyperson or spiritual leader, if any)?
- Whom do you want to participate as readers? Will there be an open time for others to share?
- Whom do you want to do your eulogy?
- Will you have people coming from a distance who need to be considered?
- Will you have a reception? Where?
- How will that be financed?
- What cultural aspects need to be taken into consideration?
- Is there a charity or a non-profit you want to receive memorial contributions?
- Do you want donations in lieu of flowers?
- What life history needs to be included in your obituary?
- What do you want to be remembered for?

Funeral home considerations:

- Which funeral home will you use?
- Can you make contact with the director in advance?
- What kind of coffin would you like?
- How will this be taken care of financially?
- Do you want a viewing or wake?
- Do you want a closed or open casket (depending on your religious tradition)?
- What clothes do you want to be buried in?
- Where will you be buried or interred?
- Do you have a plot?
- Will others in the family be buried there with you?
- If you desire to be cremated, where do you want your ashes interred or spread?
- Are you an organ donor?
- Do you want your body given to help science?

Caring for the Caregiver

Caregiving takes its toll on you. Did you know…

- ❖ "The longer a caregiver has been providing care, the more likely she or he is to report fair or poor health. Specifically, 23% of those who have been providing care for five years or more report their health is fair or poor.

- ❖ Half of caregivers (53%) say that their caregiving takes time away from friends and other family members. Those who have sacrificed this time with family and friends are far more likely to feel high emotional stress (47%) than are those who have been able to maintain the time they spend with family and friends (14%).

- ❖ As the baby boom generation ages over the next 25 years, the numbers of people needing care will swell. The numbers of younger people available to provide care are likely to dwindle. This suggests that in the future, caregivers will be older, on average, than today's caregivers and may have greater infirmity of their own. In addition, the younger people who step into a caregiving role in the future may perceive they have less choice about becoming a caregiver. A greater share of caregivers may provide care to two or more care recipients."

Source: Caregiving in the USA (Caregiving.org, AARP and MetLife 2009)

Given these statistics, it is crucial for those who are called upon to provide care for their aging parents on a part or full-time basis to become experts in SELF-care. Exercising, eating right, taking time off, knowing your limits, talking to others, spending time with your own family, and asking for help are all essential during this stressful period of time. Yet so many caregivers have difficulty taking the time they need to replenish themselves.

Many corporate employers know the value of encouraging self-care as well. In the mid-1980's many larger corporations began to offer eldercare benefits, after the model of childcare benefits. They saw how their employees who were also caregiving for family members needed extra support in order to continue to be productive at work.

A MetLife study showed, "Employed caregivers seem to be able to provide care to someone for 14 hours or less per week (considered a low level of caregiving) with little impact on their ability to stay on the job. However, providing 20 hours or more per week often results in major work adjustments, such as cutting back on hours or stopping work altogether, and the decline in annual income that goes with that work adjustment.

The well-established stresses of caregiving may lead to greater risk of chronic disease, either from the direct effects of such stress, or from the impact of caregiving (evident in poorer sleep, greater fatigue, and depression), or from less attention to one's own health (shown in lower use of preventive care, poorer diets, or less opportunity for exercise)."

Source: The MetLife Study of Working Caregivers and Employer Health Care Costs Feb 2010

Employees who report they are caregivers are at greater risk for negative behaviors such as smoking and alcohol use, and also are less likely to take care of their health. Smoking is higher among male caregivers, especially among young men. Smoking is also higher among white-collar caregivers relative to non-caregivers. Among blue-collar workers, alcohol use is higher among caregivers.

Taking care of yourself and asking for help during these stressful times is key.

❈ ❈ ❈ ❈ ❈

Regina was the primary caregiver for her husband who had Parkinson's disease. She has also helped hundreds of other caregivers going through the same thing. She has wise words. "You can't do it all. So you need to, as early as possible, recognize your strengths and the areas you think you can cope with and recognize those areas where you're just finding it too tough. It may be paperwork. It may be some of the very physical things of helping and dealing with a person (for example if they're incontinent). Try and get help with the particular areas and recognize ahead of time that you're not going to be able to handle it, or just plain don't want to handle it. Then try and look to fill those gaps by specifically asking people. Start with something small and then build up. You need to call up people and specifically say, 'Could you do this or that?' And you need to think about what their strengths are...like...could you come over and stay with Bill for a while so I can go take a break? Some people can come and do that easily. Other people you can ask to bring food. Other people you could ask to pick you up something at the store."

❈ ❈ ❈ ❈ ❈

One of my favorite books I read during a stressful period of my life is called, <u>When the Well Runs Dry</u>. Just the name of it speaks volumes. How can you continue to give if, in fact, your well has run dry? Those who continually have to dip from deep wells as caregivers need to find ways to replenish themselves so they can keep giving from resources which are full and even overflowing. Otherwise, caregiving can easily become fueled by resentment and that can lead to trouble both for yourself and for your loved one.

If you find yourself running dry for too long a period of time, you may seek professional help from a therapist, clergyperson, or other spiritual advisor. He or she can help you find support which is meaningful to you. They can offer you written materials, direct you to inner resources of meditation and prayer, lead you to respite care resources, and more.

Regina says people probably underestimate the benefits of talking to a professional. Here's her advice: "Talk to them about whatever it is. Build up some kind of relationship with ease and comfort in talking about issues. For a lot of people it's extremely hard to talk about personal things and some people are very withdrawn and restrained. It's just something they're unable to do and it really stunts the process."

In addition, most local Offices for the Aging have support networks in place for caregivers. Many groups also exist under the auspices of organizations according to diagnoses. For example, there are support groups which cater specifically to caregivers of those with Parkinson's disease, or Alzheimer's disease. Check your local listings.

Possible "invisible conversations"™ within yourself:

- When is she going to die? (Will the money last and will my sanity/energy last?)
- What is the dynamic in your household?
- Are family members talking? If not, what needs to be said to start getting things moving?
- What is/are the REAL issue(s) here?
- Are there money issues involved?
- Is there transparency about how money is handled?
- Does everyone know what is expected of them and what our aging loved one expects?

Questions for reflection for caregivers regarding self-care

- What am I feeling right now?
- Are these feelings based on real or imagined outcomes?
- What is REALLY at issue? Are these feelings based on the current situation or on childhood fears?
- Am I resentful over my newfound role? If so, what can I do to work through it now?
- Is there someone who can help me with logistics?
- Is there someone/some group who can help me with emotional support both within my family and outside of my family?
- Is my world getting too small?
- What can I do today to bring more balance into my life?

Protecting Your Loved One

Many states use the term "Vulnerable Adult" in their materials surrounding the protection of older adults from abuse. Depending on your state, the definition of a vulnerable adult may include: any person older than age 18 or emancipated by marriage that has a substantial mental or functional impairment; persons receiving services from any individual who for compensation serves as a personal aide to a person who self-directs his or her own care in his or her home; a person with health problems that place him or her in a dependent position.

Depending on your state, abuse of a vulnerable adult may include: neglect, financial exploitation, sexual or physical assault, or abandonment by a family member, care provider, or other person who has a relationship with the vulnerable adult.

Physical Abuse:

You hear stories all the time in the headlines where an adult child has neglected or beaten her aging parent for whom they have been responsible. Sometimes those incidents have tragically resulted in death. No one wants to see that happen and no one deserves to be treated that way…ever. But abuse can occur on many levels and can break families apart.

❋　❋　❋　❋　❋

Before Jerri's mother moved into a nursing home due to her progressive dementia, her sister suspected that another sister was abusing their elderly mother by isolating her and getting excessively angry with her. "My sister moved in with Mom. Mom couldn't have friends over. She changed her massage therapists, and Mom freaked out." Jerri said she also witnessed her sister's "flaring anger" and energy at her mother. She and her other sister agonized over what to do. "We can't address it because it's criminal and addressing it would (emotionally) kill my mother." They quickly decided to move their mother to an assisted living facility near Jerri as a way to resolve the issue.

❋　❋　❋　❋　❋

Physical abuse is an issue of power and control. Vulnerable adults are given that name because they don't often have the power they once did and rely on others for their needs to be met. When abuse occurs, it is a criminal offense. When someone comes upon a situation where they find potential abuse of a vulnerable adult, they should report it to their local police. Some professionals are mandated by the state to report such instances when they suspect elder abuse, just as in cases of child abuse. The law is there to protect anyone who is vulnerable in society.

Considerations if you suspect neglect or abuse:

- Does your parent have bruises or wounds which may or may not be explained?
- Does your parent complain of pain around their genital area?
- Does your parent have bed sores?
- Does your parent flinch or show fear toward any particular person...caregiver or not?
- Is your parent overly protective of anyone in particular?

Questions to ask an aging loved one/friend/ neighbor to prevent elder abuse:

- Is anything going on at home?
- Do any caregivers yell at you?
- What are the triggers that set them off?
- Are you ever afraid for your safety with anyone?
- Do you have any bruises?
- Do you need to talk to anyone privately? Clergy or another professional?
- If you could change your current caregiver, would you? Why?

Questions for self-reflection if you feel you may be at risk of causing harm:

(Note: If you find that you might be at risk of abusing your aging parent in any way, get help before it's too late. There are many resources available to support you through your local office of the aging, support groups, clergy or therapists.)

- Do I resent caring for my aging loved one? Why?
- Am I caring for myself?
- What do I need right now?
- Is there anyone who can come right now to relieve the pressure I'm feeling?
- Is there someone I can call right now to let off some of the steam I'm feeling?
- What is something I can do right now to ensure my parent's safety?
- Is there any behavior I would not want someone else to know about?
- Would someone else be treating my parent better than I am right now?

Financial Abuse:

Many scam artists continue to find ways to deceive well intentioned vulnerable adults out of countless dollars through the mail, email, or through in-person offers. Scams can wipe out any size bank account. Even the most sophisticated of investors can find themselves as the object of fraud and lose their life savings, such as in the case of clients of Bernard Madoff.

Sometimes a vulnerable adult is at risk of financial abuse by one of their own children. Several of the people I interviewed for this book suspected another adult sibling was manipulating their parent into writing them checks for their financial gain. Some adult children have manipulated or tricked their parents into signing documents they had no idea they were signing, giving away control of their assets. If this is the case, the cure is to disarm the abuser. Bring professionals into the situation, so you can get as many sets of eyes on your parent's financial affairs as possible. If the suspected person is also the power of attorney, you may need to have the court intervene and get a guardianship/conservatorship to remove his control.

Whether you are the adult child responsible for your parents' healthcare and financial matters or not, keeping alert to and asking questions about people involved with their physical, financial, and emotional health will help prevent possible abuse.

Questions to consider with your aging parent:

- Is everything going okay with (caregiver's name)?
- How does your aide get paid?
- Have you noticed if anything is missing?
- How are you feeling about how your financial affairs are being handled?
- Has anyone asked you to sign anything recently?
- Has anyone asked to provide new services for you recently?
- Read or talk about a story in the news. Did you hear about the guy who was taken advantage of? Has that ever happened to you?
- Would you feel OK about having two signatures on your account to protect your assets for your long-term care? (An attorney or financial planner may also be able to help with this question.)
- Would it be OK if your power of attorney went ahead and looked at your bank records to make sure everything is alright?

Part 4

Practical Considerations

How and When to Begin These Conversations

The sooner you can have the kind of important conversations outlined in this book with your aging parents, the better. The organization Caregiverstress.com has even coined the phrase the "40/70" Rule®. The idea being, that if you're 40, or your parents are 70, it's time to start talking. The same is true of the "70/40" Rule®. If you're 70 and your kids are 40, it's time to start talking about some of the issues of concern to older adults as they age." (For more, go to www.caregiverstress.com)

❋ ❋ ❋ ❋ ❋

Judy's father talked with her when she was in her 20's about what his and her mother's wishes were when they wouldn't be able to live on their own anymore. That was after they went through a difficult time with her aunt who needed more care but did not want to go into a nursing home. Judy says, "My father sat me down and said, 'There's going to come a day when this is going to be necessary for your mom and me (to go into a nursing home). Don't listen to anything we say (then), because we know you'll do what's right.'" Judy relied on those words after her father's death and her mother's dementia had advanced. Still, Judy struggled when her mother would say, 'I never thought my child would do this to me." However, she says knowing what her mother had said before she became ill was some comfort. After that, Judy had the same conversation with her own children, "because they watched how hard it was with my mom."

❋ ❋ ❋ ❋ ❋

Some may wait to try and have important life conversations until it's too late and their aging parents are not able to respond as they would have earlier in life due to dementia or other debilitating illnesses. If that is your situation, there are still ways you can communicate. Even though the communication is different, there are ways to express love and care in those years. Adults in the early stages of Alzheimer's disease, for example, may still be able to remember and discuss events which pull on long term memory even though they may not be able to recall more recent events. Older adults also may respond to familiar prayers, songs or familiar traditions, such as lighting candles for Shabbat.

Betty says of her mother, "She may not remember what you said, or what you did, but the memory is as much in the heart as in the mind."

Specific timing is another issue in communicating. Some families decide to have a meeting when siblings and parents are all together. They schedule these family meetings around birthdays or holiday gatherings, for example. The Internet has also made it easier for video conferencing or conference calling for updates between family members. If mom or dad is calling the meeting, the conversation may begin with something as easy as, "Why don't we all get together before/after the celebration to discuss some plans about my future?" If one of the adult children is calling the meeting because mom or dad can't for whatever reason, it might go something like this: "I'd like to call a family meeting to discuss some of Mom's increased frailty, her anticipated short and long-term needs, and the changing dynamics."

Management of open family communication is key because it keeps everyone in the loop and makes transparency possible. When siblings feel decisions are made behind closed doors, it can be a breeding ground for indirect communication and mistrust. (For more, see the section "Communicating with Siblings") Family meetings also provide the opportunity for everyone to be a part of the caregiving decisions and the discussion of the division of responsibilities.

It is important to plan for uncertainty before a crisis forces bad decisions. The person who takes mom or dad to the hospital may not be the one who is the health care proxy, for example. Timely conversations are about helping mom or dad explore realistic options to deal with the uncertainty both in the short and long-term, and then updating and adjusting as the needs change.

(Note: In case of an emergency, hospital staff, social workers, chaplains, attorneys, and other caregivers can help facilitate conversations so that the appropriate decisions are made in a timely manner.)

Why Some Conversations Are Invisible

If you are having relevant conversations with your aging parents, congratulations! If not, don't worry, you're not alone. While delving into the important topics which may or may not have been lurking in the shadows, you may discover many obstacles to having conversations about difficult life transitions.

A study out of Nationwide Insurance company states:

"While more than two-thirds of Americans say they understand the value of having conversations about difficult topics ranging from estate planning to sex, they also reveal a strong impulse to tell white lies, screen calls, ignore e-mails, and even find a place to hide in an effort to avoid them."

Avoidance has a high price. Those who engage in avoidance, report loss of: sleep, financial security, health and even relationships in startling numbers.

(Nationwide Tough Talks Survey 2007, Nationwide.com)

So, what are some of the obstacles to communicating clearly and effectively with your aging parents?

A. Loss of Cognitive Function and Other Abilities

Communicating in general, may be more difficult as a person ages, affecting the type and quality of communication they are able to have. According to the Brookings Institute, older adults tend to experience declines in cognitive function. "About half of the population between ages 80 and 89 either has dementia or a diagnosis of 'cognitive impairment without dementia.'" (www.brookings.edu) However, that statistic also means that 50% of older adults experience no cognitive decline.

While cognition varies from individual to individual, there is a trend. Some people begin to show more pronounced cognitive decline earlier and some later. Other diagnoses may interact with existing decline and exacerbate the older adult's ability to function as he once did. Hearing loss, visual impairment, physical impairments, medications, social isolation, and dehydration may also make a person appear as demented when they are not.

If you suspect any type of memory impairment, it is important to understand the effect on capacity for decision making. That shift may make meaningful conversation a bit more difficult for both of you. Gerontologist Sue Belisle says, "Without short term memory, an individual does not have the capacity to have a conversation and will immediately forget. Communication must be basic, simple, and will be generally unreliable."

❀ ❀ ❀ ❀ ❀

Jenny saw her mother decline and moved her to an assisted living facility near her. But she says the process was agonizing for them both. "It hurts to watch her like this. This is loss of her mind and she knows it and it's scary and it's sad."

❀ ❀ ❀ ❀ ❀

Sandy, a 75 year old says, "People say they're fine because of pride or privacy." While her cognitive abilities are still intact, Sandy's hearing decline makes her anxious when she's around bigger groups, including big family gatherings. She says she gets overwhelmed at all of the noise. At times, she has made the choice to withdraw.

❀ ❀ ❀ ❀ ❀

B. Fear

Fear is a major inhibitor in life, in general. It keeps you from doing the things you need to do or prompts you to do things you don't want to do. If faced with the effects of aging in one or both of your parents, you may not want to confront the frailty you see.

Mary says, "You don't talk about this stuff. If you do, you would take something away from them...their hope, their belief that they need to live the way they were living." And so, out of respect for the relationship, you might not say anything. Fear keeps you stuck.

You may have fear of your parent's death whether it's approaching or years down the road. In either case, the death of a loved one may be new territory for you. You and your parents may not know what to expect, and it's normal to have some fear of the unknown. There are many people who can help you at all points of the journey ahead.

C. Denial

Denial is a lack of acknowledgment that a situation exists. It can be an obstacle to communication for both the aging adult as well as the adult child. Professors Kenneth Mitchell and Herbert Anderson say, "We are still anxious and angry in the face of human limitations. We do not want to be reminded that someday we shall die. We do not even like to think we are aging. Every loss and separation in life is an intimation of mortality. We protest because we do not like being limited." (Used with permission from the publisher, Westminster John Knox Press.)

Denial is an important psychological defense. People with early stages of dementia or another diagnosis may exhibit denial over the fact that their condition is getting worse. Larry Blaker, of The Senior Life Options, works with many families at this stage of life. He says in some cases, "An adult with dementia will waiver and think it's the other spouse who has the problem." A mother who's experiencing early stages of dementia may say something to the effect of, "Your dad is being inappropriate." In that situation, the adult child or responsible caregiver needs to make sure an assessment of cognitive ability is made by a healthcare professional. If capacity has been impaired, the ability to break through the older adult's denial may never happen.

❀ ❀ ❀ ❀ ❀

Jessie says even though her mother probably had been dealing with the early stages of Alzheimer's disease for quite some time, she had a fierce fear of the loss of independence. On top of that, her father was in denial over her mother's problem. "My mother was not allowing anyone to clean the house. She became very paranoid. She would not let anyone to come and help her. She was really unable to care for herself." Jessie says she only came upon her mother's condition after her father got ill. It suddenly came to light that he had been covering up her mother's condition for some time.

❀ ❀ ❀ ❀ ❀

As the adult child, you may also be in denial that your parent is declining and getting closer to death so you avoid any conversation about preparations for end of life.

❀ ❀ ❀ ❀ ❀

Paula, who is currently very healthy says, "Not one of my children wants to hear about my possibly dying." They say to her, "What do you mean you're old!! Stop saying that!" Paula wonders "What should Mama say to her grown up ducklings to get them to be realistic about the passing of time?" They think "I should live forever."

The problem with denial is that when decisions are avoided during healthy times, a family loses the opportunity to find out the answers to important questions which need to be answered. The decisions may then be forced upon them when a crisis hits. So, while family members are dealing with grief or fear in the midst of the crisis, they also must deal with details which may affect the final days of their parents' lives. The alternative is to live with the consequences of not making them.

❀ ❀ ❀ ❀ ❀

Jimmy says he had been somewhat in denial of his mother's illness. He didn't have a conversation with her during her final days about whether she wanted to be buried or cremated. After her death, Jimmy's father made the decision to have her cremated. As a result, he says he felt guilty, because he knows she would have wanted to have been buried based on her family's cultural traditions.

❀ ❀ ❀ ❀ ❀

D. Black Holes and Estrangement

Have you ever known a family with members who cut off communication with other family members for a days, weeks, or even years? These periods are what some refer to as communication "black holes." They usually don't exist in a vacuum. Patterns of estrangement with black holes within a family may be traced back for generations. They may occur for a variety of reasons. Sometimes a child feels he can't grow or maintain a sense of who he is while still maintaining connection with other family members. Sometimes black holes occur as a result of trauma experienced either at the hands of a parent or another responsible person. In other cases, people may separate themselves from family connection or be forced out because of mental illness or addiction.

Estrangement occurs when there is alienation in a relationship. Communication may continue, but there is a break in the loving connection. In family life not everyone may experience estrangement in the same way. Children experience family life differently. The dynamics which wound one don't bother another. So, if alienation occurs, not all children will be estranged from the family at the same time, if at all.

Black holes and estrangement can leave a family dysfunctional and stuck in patterns for years.

❊ ❊ ❊ ❊ ❊

Becky says her childhood household was always very dramatic. She remembers having been asked at age five or six if she listened on the radio to soap operas and replying, "No, my family's stories are always more interesting." Her mother, Marnie, was married three times and had children by each husband. Throughout her early years, each of the children was sent to live elsewhere with relatives because Becky says they were "too much" for her mother. Marnie became ill in her 30's and lived with debilitating pain for the remaining 46 years of her life. Becky says her mother used her illness as a way to manipulate her children and make them feel guilty for not doing more to help her. Nearly a decade before her death, Becky talked with Marnie on the phone. She says her mother tried to lay another guilt trip on her for not doing more to help. Becky says, "I made a conscious decision not to talk to her (after that). I didn't need any more family drama." As a single mom with four young children of her own at the time, Becky says, "I knew I couldn't do any more for my mother." She said she left the ball in her mother's court to make the next call…and they never talked again.

❊ ❊ ❊ ❊ ❊

Black holes and estrangement can affect the ways in which aging adults face their futures.

One attorney estimates a whopping 40% of the families she deals with in her Estates and Trusts firm have a family member who is estranged, many times because of some form of mental illness. "There's sometimes some reluctance to deal with that issue, to talk about that issue with the other children in a meaningful way. Sometimes it's because the parent feels guilty that they somehow were responsible for the child not communicating with them or possibly hating them. For whatever reason, it's hard for them to tell us (their attorney). Sometimes it's hard for them to talk about it with their spouse."

E. Lack of forgiveness

Forgiveness is the process of letting go of pain, resentment or anger experienced as a result of a perceived wrong by another person or people. It may be formally given in words, or through actions. Forgiveness is powerful and can be given immediately or over a long period of time in stages. When a person still lives in the pain of the past, they may experience a lack of inner freedom, which may create a barrier to communication with others.

Jane was nearing the end of her life. One of Jane's sons, named Jeff, never visited and rarely talked with her during her dying process. When he did, there was great struggle and the conversations ended up leaving Jeff feeling great frustration and anger. Jeff had never forgiven his mother for the ways she had treated his father during his life and blamed her for making the family dysfunctional. Holding onto those feelings created difficulty for Jeff in many of his adult relationships.

Forgiveness is an opportunity not only to set yourself free from the past, but the other person as well. It doesn't mean forgetting what happened to cause the pain, but it enables you to move on from the blame and resentment which may be holding you hostage and keeping you from living more fully.

A therapist once told me, "If you hold onto resentment with someone longer than 24 hours, chances are it relates to your family of origin." As an adult, if you are holding back forgiveness from your aging parent, it's most likely also affecting some aspect of your current life.

Janet says she didn't realize that the deep seeded feelings of hurt she had buried for the 20 years since her mother's death were still affecting her on some level. As she discussed her own aging process with her adult daughter, it was clear that she was still holding onto feelings about events which were decades old. Her daughter told her, "Just because you ignore the past, doesn't mean it will go away. Imagine how much energy it takes to hold all of those feelings deep inside."

If you find you have not forgiven someone, the good news is that you can change the flow of the tide at any moment. Forgiveness can open up new areas inside yourself for love, compassion and peace.

Letting go of the obstacles. Try This:

Sometimes obstacles and the reactions to them are set in place for a very good reason. The reason may have been good when you first encountered it, but you may have outgrown it. It may no longer serve its purpose in your life. Find a quiet place where you can do this exercise. Take a few minutes to write out your answers to the following statements:

❖ Think about barriers that are holding you back from having a better relationship with your parents and siblings.

❖ Some of the obstacles that prevent me from more effective communication with my parents and family are _____, _____, and _____.

❖ I believe the breakdown in communication originated when

_____.

❖ I think the situation can be improved if

_____.

❖ I can help resolve this by

_____.

❖ This obstacle may have affected these relationships

_____, _____.

❖ In the face of your current circumstances, are you ready to let go of the obstacle to the best of your ability? _____. If no, why not? _____.
If yes, when will you make a positive move forward? _____.

❖ How will you know if the obstacle is no longer present?

Next Steps

The inner shift which occurs when you care for those who once cared for you is monumental. It may take all the inner resources you have. The transition into the caregiving role requires an extraordinary presence of mind and spirit. When "invisible conversations"™ exist in those relationships, the ability to be present and to embrace the person whom you have called "parent" is diminished or may be blocked all together.

Bringing "invisible conversations"™ to the surface in your relationships often takes courage and strength. Speaking the truth in love and with compassion creates a powerful, life-giving force. That force shines light into areas which may have remained in the shadows until now. But that light acts as a powerful beacon and has the chance to heal relationships which may have been broken in some way. People relax in a new way and confusion is decreased. While it may feel scary to bring something forth which has been unspoken for so long, the action you take may heal your soul and the soul of the other person. A new connection is forged. Finally, when you take a risk and step out into the creative world with courage to bring those "invisible conversations"™ to light, breaking through perceived boundaries, you have the chance to honor yourself and to live more nobly in the world.

If you have not done so, now is the time to act.

- Begin the conversations with your parents to find out what they need and want in the days, months and years ahead.

- If they need assistance, talk with an attorney, with a financial advisor, or with those who can help you in the caregiving role. If changes need to be made to your previous care plans, sit down and make adjustments with family members or trusted advisors.

- Don't do this alone. Find support for yourself either through a support group or with family members. Take time to replenish yourself daily. Laugh a lot, love a lot so you can live a lot.

May your sweetest days be ahead of you.

Shannon White

Resources

Advance Directives:

Five Wishes; This is a widely-used resource for planning advance directives through the non-profit Aging With Dignity (found at www.agingwithdignity.org.). The topics are: The Person I Want to Make Care Decisions for Me When I Can't; The Kind of Medical Treatment I Want or Don't Want; How Comfortable I Want to Be; How I Want People to Treat Me; What I Want My Loved Ones to Know. The topics covered in the document are excellent beginning places to continue conversations. Each section has a list of wants and desires and the participants cross out those they do not wish to have as part of their own care. There is also a space for additional written comments. Five Wishes does not include a DNR or a power of attorney for financial matters (only medical power of attorney/health care agent). It is also not a last will and testament.

The cost is minimal: $5 per copy. The price decreases if you order over a certain number of copies. A CD is also available, and a wallet card is provided so caregivers will know you have documents on file. Five Wishes is available in 26 languages.

Also check with your Attorney General's office website for your state's unique regulations. Oftentimes, the websites provide documents for immediate download and use free-of-charge.

Books, Articles, and Brochures

Basics of Alzheimer's disease: What it is and what you can do, Alzheimer's Association, 2010. For more information see www.alz.org.

How to Help an Older Driver: A Guide for Planning Safe Transportation
This free 26-page booklet/download is an excellent resource for having the discussion about driving with dignity and respect. http://www.aaafoundation.org/pdf/ODlarge.pdf

MetLife Mature Market Survey: *2011 Mature Market Survey of Long-term Care Costs* http://www.metlife.com/mmi/research/2011-market-survey-long-term-care-costs.html#findings

Mitchell, Kenneth and Herbert Anderson, <u>All Our Losses, All Our Griefs, Resources for Pastoral Care</u>, (Westminster Press, Philadelphia, 1983).

Preventing Family Clashes When Caring For An Aging Loved One (Patch posted by Elizabeth Crenson Sept 1, 2011) Anthony J. Enea, Esq. Anthony J. Enea is managing partner of the firm Enea, Scanlan & Sirignano, LLP

Smart Brain, Strong Brain, Fit Brain: The Quality of Good Mental Health...A Handbook for Older Adults (Kaufman, Sylvia, Suzanne Belisle, PhD, Celia Juris, Kate Zisman)

2010, Mental Health Association of Rockland County, NY. For more, go to: www.smartbrainstrongbrain.com

The Age of Reason: Financial Decisions Over the Life Cycle With Implications for Regulation; http://www.brookings.edu/~/media/Files/Programs/ES/BPEA/2009_fall_bpea _papers/2009_fall_bpea_agarwal.pdf .

Organizations:

www.caregiverstress.com
www.caregiving.org
www.seniorlifeoptions.net
www.niaaa.nih.gov (National Institute on Alcohol Abuse and Alcoholism)

Other Resources:

Movie: The Ultimate Gift" (2007, 20th Century Fox) 1 hour 57 minutes; Rated PG and based on Jim Stovall's best-selling book. Starring: James Garner, Brian Dennehy, Abigail Breslin, Drew Fuller, Ali Hillis, Bill Cobbs.

Acknowledgements

This book would not have been possible without the love, experience and support of many people:

My readers: Liz Hunt, Rhona Johnson, and Sue Belisle gave wonderful and insightful suggestions in their areas of expertise; my editor, Wendy VanHatten, of vhwritingservices.com, utilized her skills and wisdom to provide a readable text; my formatter and cover designer, Peter Biadasz of Total Publishing and Media (www.totalpublishingand media.com) provided the beauty and aesthetics.

Thank you to advisors Rev. Dr. Martin Montonye, and Vincent Molina for their guidance, encouragement and suggestions. Thank you to Larry Blaker, of Senior Life Options, and to Michael Amoruso, Esq., for their work and expertise. Thank you to Bernie Dohrman, who provided the inspiration for my brand, "The Invisible Conversations"™. Thank you to Steve Harrison, James Malinchak and Alex Mandossian for stimulating marketing ideas. Thank you to Nancy Collamer, who provided encouragement during the writing process.

And thank you to the many people, both aging adults and adult children, who shared their heart-felt stories with me for this book. Your courage and honesty in the face of great challenges leave me inspired.

www.TotalPublishingAndMedia.com

About the Author

S hannon White is a nationally acclaimed speaker, Emmy-nominated TV reporter, and Presbyterian clergywoman living in New York. She and her daughter, Peyton are also the authors of How as School Today? Fine (available through Amazon.com and at www.shannonawhite.com). The audio and e-book version are now available under the brand, The Invisible Conversations between You and Your Children at www.shannonawhite.com/invisible-conversations.

Through her brand, "The Invisible Conversations"™, Shannon seeks to assist people to have authentic, open conversations in all areas of their lives. Other titles under her brand are currently in production.

Shannon has spoken at Fortune 500 companies, and organizations as well as at small group retreats. If you would like more information on how to bring Shannon to your business or organization, please visit us at www.shannonawhite.com or email her at info@shannonawhite.com.

A percentage of the sales of this book will be donated to help fund Alzheimer's research and support programs. To learn more about Alzheimer's disease, go to www.Alz.org.

CPSIA information can be obtained at www.ICGtesting.com
Printed in the USA
LVOW031343030712

288728LV00009B/5/P